Auditions Undressed

by

Daniel Bowling

ISBN: 978-0-9561491-0-7

For information please address:

auditionsundressed@danielbowling.co.uk

"Having worked with Daniel Bowling first hand, I can tell you that reading this book will clarify exactly what auditioning is all about and how to be fully prepared for that one chance to show what you can do! A great and honest read!"

Lee Mead

Star of West End's Joseph and the Amazing Technicolor Dreamcoat and Winner of BBC's 'Any Dream Will Do.'

"A valuable book about auditioning expressed in a clear and direct form that all actors or performers from within the industry that must face those tough auditions can draw strength."

Denise Van Outen

International television and theatre star and celebrity judge on BBC's 'Any Dream Will Do' and 'I'd Do Anything.'

"Auditioning can be one of the most nerve-racking and frightening experiences for any actor whether new to the business or a veteran. 'Auditions Undressed' by Daniel Bowling is an invaluable tool for performers everywhere to be best prepared for the all-important auditioning process."

David Ian

International Producer and celebrity judge on BBC's 'How Do You Solve A Problem Like Maria?', 'You're the One That We Want' and ITV's 'Grease is the Word'.

Contents

Acknowledgements

Boundless thanks to my wife Grainne Renihan who made many invaluable contributions to this book and continues to be my greatest inspiration as well as the best singer I know. And to my son Ciaran, who seems to instinctively know everything in this book and more already – watch out world!

Thanks to Lizzy Shaw for her beautiful modeling for the cover and to her husband Luke Shaw for his brilliant cover photographs.

Many thanks to Satya Olgilvy, Mike Townsend, and the theatre staff at Her Majesty's Theatre, part of the Really Useful Theatre Group, for their permission and help in taking the cover photos.

Thanks to Louise Riordan, Nial Riordan, and Nick Coupe for their invaluable help in proofreading and editing text as well as their generous encouragement.

Many thanks to John Alastair for his formatting expertise and endless patience.

And most especially thanks to the thousands of actors and singers I've had the privilege to audition over the past 15 years – I've tried to never take your courage for granted!

Forward

Over the course of many years as a performer, coach, and conductor, I've come to the conclusion that as much as I'd like to, I can't teach anyone anything. I can encourage, guide, cajole, or at best inspire, but I ultimately can't teach someone how to sing in tune or deliver a lyric truthfully. Each individual must discover these mysteries by and for themselves.

Auditions prove to be a curse for many a talented soul. To stare into the face of likely rejection day in and day out as the only means to employment in the field that you love can be soul destroying and ultimately your worst enemy. My main purpose in writing this book was to hopefully provide a simple resource that would inspire a bit of confidence and provoke a bit more thought towards preparing for those ever-crucial auditions.

For each chapter, I have tried to include quotations that will actually continue the exploration of the theme and not merely blindly support the premise of the chapter. Nothing is ever black and white in the arts and my sincere hope is that this modest little book will be inspirational and not dogmatic.

Although nothing replaces talent and instinct, sometimes the smallest seed of an idea can quicken unfulfilled potential and arouse new curiosities. 'A mighty flame followeth a tiny spark.' I hope you find it useful.

Daniel Bowling

1
Choose Material You Can Wear

Choosing material that fits who you are and where your abilities lie is crucial to giving a convincing audition and getting that much needed recall. When you choose material that fits you like a glove, it not only enables you to connect with the song or monologue more intuitively, but it really tells the audition panel that you've done your homework and that you know who you are and where you're going as an artist.

Theatrical repertoire always has a context; whatever song or monologue you choose will come from a specific character, with a specific age, gender, shape, status, story and vocal range. Choosing material from a character that doesn't approximately correspond with your own character is dangerous ground for auditions. When choosing your monologue or song, don't deny who you are or exactly where your abilities lie. Whatever material you choose should roughly come from a character that could fit a description of you. Think about it – the vast majority of productions are cast to type. It takes a courageous or, some may argue, stupid director to take a chance and cast against type or in some cases, years of history. Even for new productions, the blueprint for characters often becomes set early on in the process, often in workshops, before the first casting even takes place.

This is not to suggest for one moment that you shouldn't learn and explore material that isn't a perfect match with who you are. Quite the contrary, taking on characters that stretch you as an actor is vital for your development, but think twice before doing it for an audition. Getting that recall is tough enough. Choosing material that doesn't marry with who and what you are is asking for trouble. Keep the picture clear and don't confuse us – we're not that bright you know!

"We are always more anxious to be distinguished for a talent which we do not possess, than to be praised for the fifteen which we do possess."
Mark Twain (1835 –1910), Mark Twain's Autobiography

"With any part you play, there is a certain amount of yourself in it. There has to be, otherwise it's just not acting. It's lying."
Johnny Depp, (1963 –)

"Make the best use of what is in your power, and take the rest as it happens."
Epictetus (55 AD –135 AD)

"Use what talents you possess: the woods would be very silent if no birds sang there except those that sang best."
Henry Van Dyke (1852 – 1933)

"Most people would succeed in small things if they were not troubled with great ambitions."
Henry Wadsworth Longfellow (1807 –1882), Driftwood; Table Talk, 1857

"Common sense is the best sense I know of."
Lord Chesterfield (1694 – 1773)

"True luck consists not in holding the best of the cards at the table; luckiest is he who knows just when to rise and go home."
John Hay (1838 –1905), Distichs, latter 19th century

"The best things carried to excess are wrong."
Charles Churchill (1656 – 1714)

2
Preparation Prevails

It seems so obvious, but I have to ask you, how well have you prepared? What do you do on a daily basis to encourage a nimble mind and a healthy body? What consistent measures do you have in place to improve your craft so when your agent calls saying, "You have an audition tomorrow morning. Here's the address," you don't find yourself crippled with fear at the mere contemplation of going?

When was the last time you took a singing lesson? When was the last time you attended an acting workshop? When was the last time you went to the gym? When was the last time you did mock runs of your audition material for colleagues, fellow students, friends or family?

And by the way, being 'in work' doesn't somehow exclude you from the necessities of ongoing preparation. In fact, when experienced actors complain to me about castings getting younger and younger, I regretfully have to explain that one of the reasons for this is that drama students are, by a huge majority, the ones who are actively still in training. Are you?

So often when I ask people what they do to prepare for an audition, they tell me what they've done in the last couple of days rather than the last couple of years. In the shadow of television shows like the X Factor, where wannabe stars expect to get from A to Z without covering any of the letters in between, it is inevitable that hard graft gets replaced by hard luck!

I compare taking an audition to the 100 metre sprint. The world record currently stands at 9.69 seconds run by Jamaican born Usain Bolt. Bolt holds the Olympic and world records for the 100 metres, the 200 metres and, along with his teammates, the 4x 100 metres relay all set recently at the 2008 Beijing Olympics. If you don't want your audition to last less than 9.69 seconds, then I beg of you to put some thought, actually a lot of thought, into what systems, what methodology Usain Bolt has in place to run faster than any other man on earth in all three sprinting events. It's not the preparation he puts in days before a competition that wins him races, it's simply the focused, intelligent and consistent hard graft over years that makes him and will make you, the best. Preparation always prevails!

"It usually takes more than three weeks to prepare a good impromptu speech."
Mark Twain (1835 –1910)

"The future belongs to those who prepare for it today."
Malcolm X (1925 –1965)

"It is better to look ahead and prepare than to look back and regret."
Jackie Joyner-Kersee (1962 –)

"I say luck is when an opportunity comes along, and you're prepared for it."
Denzel Washington (1954 –)

"Confidence is preparation. Everything else is beyond your control."
Richard Kline (1944 –)

"It's what you learn after you know it all that counts"
Attributed to Harry S. Truman (1884-1972)

3
Build a Team

No artist, whether they admit it or not, has ever achieved success without the benefit of a team that has nurtured, instructed, strengthened and sustained their talents and ambition all the way up the ladder of fortune. Building a team to steer and advise your progress should be a conscious undertaking rather than a haphazard effort. The formation of your team should be the equivalent of casting your own production of the best new show in town, aptly titled, 'Success!' in which you play the starring role. Each member of that team needs to complement the others, so that everyone is collectively working in tandem towards a singular goal – your success!

First things first; skill. Find the best singing teacher you can afford and schedule regular lessons. Find out which studios offer acting workshops and audition master classes and regularly participate. Find the best dance teachers you can in a variety of styles and routinely take class. Consistently schedule mock auditions for yourself, inviting a panel of supportive friends, family and colleagues. Find a good dialect coach to employ so when an audition rides on your ability to use a particular accent successfully, you can!

Secondly, psychology. Find mentors that you can regularly call upon for counsel and encouragement. Identify and use those friends and family that best support your wish to achieve your goals and remember that this might not necessarily consist of the ones that tell you what you want to hear. Seek out at least one person who can help train you to achieve tranquillity, stillness and calm when you most need it.

Thirdly, image. You need a hairdresser who is aware of all the current trends in theatre, television and film. You need a photographer who knows what type of headshots casting directors want for each separate discipline. You need a trainer to help build your fitness levels up so strength and physique are never an issue in any casting you take. You need an objective advisor to help you choose a wardrobe that subtly compliments your best physical attributes who is not your Mom.

By using your imagination and diverse skills as an actor, you should be able to do the vast majority of the above on a budget. And if you're currently in a drama course, all the more reason to start building your team now –you won't be in school forever. Cast your team conscientiously and together you will be unstoppable!

"Players win games, teams win championships."
Bill Taylor (1949 –)

"The speed of the boss is the speed of the team."
Lee Iacocca (1924 –)

"Life is like a dogsled team. If you ain't the lead dog, the scenery never changes."
Lewis Grizzard (1946 – 1994)

"There's nothing wrong with staying small. You can do big things with a small team."
Jason Fried, (1970 –) Keynote Speech, SXSW 2006

"People don't have to like or support you, so you always have to say thank you."
Ruben Studdard (1978 –) Seventeen Magazine, September 2003

4
Technique Serves Art

Developing a strong and resilient technique as a performer is vital to success. Instincts and intuition have a somewhat finite path on their own, but when supported by a solid technique, they can become exponentially more powerful. And how do you achieve a strong technique? You might have heard the joke about the tourist in New York asking a passer-by, 'How do I get to Carnegie Hall?' to which the stranger heavily replies, "Practice! Practice!" Consistent and dedicated practice is the only way to attain that prized technique you so desire, but at the same time, practice doesn't always make perfect unless it engages the imagination as well. Although practice, and a lot of it, can help you achieve a good technique, without imagination your countless hours of work will only result in an inflexible and mundane technique. Mere repetition without focus, thought, and inspiration creates a technique built on very shaky foundations indeed where muscularity and tension will prevail and habit and routine supersede inventiveness and innovation.

In my experience, I have found that the best artists don't necessarily 'practice' as much as probe for solutions. They find a quiet, private, safe environment in order to explore, experiment, ramble, research, investigate, bend, twist, zigzag, wander, sample, taste and then put to the test. But in order to do this, you must grant yourself the time and space to be free. So often I hear or see artists practicing a song, monologue, or dance routine as if it were a race to the finish or a lesson in self-flagellation. They muscle their learning fast and furiously and never stop to smell the roses or taste the honey. Practicing that scene time and time again or singing that difficult passage a hundred times over will achieve nothing without brainwork and wit.

The pursuit of technique must never become all-consuming. Technique is only there to serve art. Remember and trust that your body has the most amazing capacity to do whatever it is you want it to do so long as the inspiration is strong enough and the visualization clear enough.

"Great dancers are not great because of their technique, they are great because of their passion."

Martha Graham (1894 –1991)

"The mere mechanical technique of acting can be taught, but the spirit that is to give life to lifeless forms must be born in a man. No dramatic college can teach its pupils to think or to feel. It is Nature who makes our artists for us, though it may be Art who taught them their right mode of expression."

Oscar Wilde (1854 – 1900)

"I would visualize things coming to me. It would just make me feel better. Visualization works if you work hard. That's the thing. You can't just visualize and go eat a sandwich."

Jim Carrey (1962 –) Oprah Winfrey Show, 1997

"In science as in love, too much concentration on technique can often lead to impotence."

P. L. Berger (1929 –)

"Take chances, make mistakes. That's how you grow. Pain nourishes your courage. You have to fail in order to practice being brave."

Mary Tyler Moore (1936 –)

5
No Excuses

Are you sick of hearing excuses? SO ARE THE AUDITION PANEL! Did you forget your music on the train? NO ONE CARES! Did you fall off your bicycle and twist your ankle on the way to the audition? NEXT! Were you struck down with the worst case you've ever had of Pharyngitis, Laryngitis, Can't-Get-Out-of-Beditis? GO BACK TO SLEEP! Your agent gave you the wrong address and time for your audition? TALK TO THE HAND! No one told you to bring in two contrasting songs? WHATEVER! You just broke up with your partner? WHY TELL US? You were mugged on your way in? DON'T PUSH IT!

If you're not ready or well enough to be at the audition, DON'T GO! If you feel you've been given an unfair amount of time to prepare, KEEP IT TO YOURSELF! If the audition panel is any good at what they do, they'll see you've twisted your ankle and hear you've got a bad throat as quickly as they'll recognize a grossly exaggerated excuse or outright lie. Besides, witnessing an actor struggle through or conquer some legitimate adversity whilst auditioning can tell us volumes about their character and potential. WHY RUIN IT BY GIVING US AN EXCUSE?

A certain amount of stoicism is required to be an actor simply because bad things sometimes happen to good people. Maybe you did lose your music on the train or maybe your agent did give you the wrong information, but make the decision to either dust yourself off and carry on with courage and dignity or go home. BUT NEVER, EVER MAKE EXCUSES! EXCUSES EQUAL FAILURE!

"We excuse our sloth under the pretext of difficulty."

Marcus Fabius Quintilian Quintilian (35 A.D. – 100 A. D.)

"The trick is not how much pain you feel —but how much joy you feel. Any idiot can feel pain. Life is full of excuses to feel pain, excuses not to live, excuses, excuses, excuses."

Erica Jong (1942 –)

"Ninety-nine percent of all failures come from people who have the habit of making excuses."

George Washington Carver (1864 –1943)

"He that is good for making excuses is seldom good for anything else."

Benjamin Franklin (1706 –1790)

"It is wise to direct your anger towards problems – - not people; to focus your energies on answers – - not excuses."

William Arthur Ward (1921 – 1994)

"No one ever excused his way to success."

Dave Del Dotto

"Excuses are the tools with which persons with no purpose in view build for themselves great monuments of nothing."

Steve Grayhm (1981 –)

6
Embrace Your Fear

Fears and self-limiting beliefs are often magnified in the days, hours and minutes before stepping through that door to begin your audition. Any number of fantasized outcomes appear real in your mind's eye. "I'll forget my words and look an idiot. My mouth will dry up and I'll sound like an old witch. My friends will get a recall and I won't. I look fat and ugly and they'll laugh at the prospect of hiring someone like me. Everyone before me sounds so good, so confident! What business do I have coming here? I'm not good enough. I'll make a fool out of myself! RUN!!!" Sound familiar?

Are you going to allow fear to stop you from achieving what you want? Are you going to allow fear to embitter you towards the profession you love? Or are you going to embrace your fear and use it to focus your mind and energize your body? Fight fire with fire. Fight the power of your emotions with the power of your mind. Remember that fear tells us we're experiencing something new, something unexpected, something exciting.

Fear heightens our senses and allows us to perform miracles. Fear reminds us that we're alive and kicking and ready to rock and roll! Fear transforms into exhilaration when you concentrate on the pleasure that confronting the fear will bring and the inevitable pain that will result if you stay within your comfort zone. Lack of action and avoidance only magnify our fears. Something wonderful will be waiting for you the more you take the plunge. Step into the void and embrace your fear.

"Courage is resistance to fear, mastery of fear —not absence of fear."
Mark Twain (1835 – 1910)

"The greatest mistake you can make in life is to be continually fearing you will make one."
Elbert Hubbard (1856 –1915)

"Nothing in life is to be feared, it is only to be understood. Now is the time to understand more, so that we may fear less."
Marie Curie (1867 – 1934)

"Do not fear to be eccentric in opinion, for every opinion now accepted was once eccentric."
Bertrand Russell (1872 – 1970)

"None but a coward dares to boast that he has never known fear."
Ferdinand Foch (1851 –1929)

"Courage can't see around corners, but goes around them anyway."
Mignon McLaughlin (1913 –1983), The Neurotic's Notebook, 1960

"Courage is not simply one of the virtues, but the form of every virtue at the testing point."
C.S. Lewis (1898-1963)

"Courage is fear holding on a minute longer."
George Smith Patton (1885-1945)

7
We Are Not the Enemy

Most audition panels consist of a diverse group of people, and can comprise any combination of the following: Directors, Writers, Orchestrators, Choreographers, Dance Captains, Resident Directors, Music Supervisors, Music Directors, Producers and Production Administrators. The balance of power and influence within each group can vary from casting to casting. Another way of describing this same group might be to say that most audition panels might consist of raging alcoholics, four time divorcees, dyspraxic nerds, control freaks, power starved mediocrities, mad fans, pompous gits, failed classical musicians, megalomaniacs, and paper pushers! In other words, human beings just like you and just as likely to make the wrong decision on the day as you are to forget your words. THEY ARE NOT THE ENEMY! DON'T TREAT THEM AS SUCH!

I've never sat on a panel where we have wished for failed auditions. We want you to do your best. We want you to shine. We want to cast you. We want to be in each other's company for the least amount of time possible. You can best help us by being fabulous! I can't tell you the number of times we audition prospective candidates with chips the size of boulders resting firmly on both shoulders and with body language that screams: "Screw you, you stupid assholes if you don't give me the *~#>ing job." We're a relatively sensitive bunch as a rule and this kind of attitude won't get you far. Concern yourself only with your behaviour and not ours – most panel's deportment can degenerate quickly as the day wears on. Don't take our antics as a cue to misbehave yourself. Instead, take pity on us and try to understand that our limited attention span is often taxed to its limit during the course of most audition periods.

Putting the shoe on the other foot can often go a long way towards securing that first job.

"Human beings, by changing the inner attitudes of their minds, can change the outer aspects of their lives."

William James (1842 – 1910)

"Could we change our attitude, we should not only see life differently, but life itself would come to be different. Life would undergo a change of appearance because we ourselves had undergone a change in attitude."

Katherine Mansfield (1888 – 1923)

"If you don't like something, change it. If you can't change it, change your attitude. Don't complain."

Maya Angelou (1928 –)

"Adopting the right attitude can convert a negative stress into a positive one."

Dr. Hans Selye (1907 – 1982)

"Ability is what you're capable of doing. Motivation determines what you do. Attitude determines how well you do it."

Lou Holtz (1937 –)

"I don't like that man. I must get to know him better."

Abraham Lincoln (1809 – 1865)

"Wherever you go, no matter what the weather, always bring your own sunshine."

Anthony J. D'Angelo (1972 –), The College Blue Book, 1995

"Life is a shipwreck but we must not forget to sing in the lifeboats."

Voltaire (1694 – 1778)

8
Professionalism

When applying for a job, each occupation has its own set of practices and customs which define professional behaviour and the theatre business is no exception. Where most businesses would expect a prospective employee to arrive for their interview in a suit and tie, we usually find it quite terrifying. Most companies might view acting, singing or dancing in an interview as a wee bit eccentric, but for us, it's bloody compulsory.

Having said that, there are certain principles which apply universally when seeking employment, whatever the job may be. Since some theatre artists I know wouldn't know a principle from a pirouette I suggest you have a little look at the below. I hope these tips prove useful whether it's for an audition for Little Shop of Horrors or just an interview for the little shop round the corner.

- Write a CV that is concise, current, simple to read and completely truthful.
- Be early.
- Wear attire that is appropriate and respectful to the occasion.
- Listen carefully and enthusiastically.
- Think before you speak. Speak clearly, confidently, and truthfully.
- Make eye contact when speaking.
- Smile from time to time.
- Ask intelligent questions.
- Respond warmly but not with over familiarity.
- Use body language that conveys poise, capability and confidence.
- Accept and breathe into your nerves.
- Use humour with extreme prejudice.
- Know as much as you can about the company you're applying to and the persons who will be conducting your interview/audition.

- Know what role you're being considered for and prepare your material thoroughly.
- Carry extra CV's with you.
- Anticipate any questions likely to be asked and know your answers.
- If you don't understand a question, ask for clarification.
- Don't smoke, swear, self-deprecate, criticize or fidget in or anywhere near the location of your interview/audition.

Happy job hunting!

"A professional is a person who can do his best at a time when he doesn't particularly feel like it."
Alistair Cooke (1908 – 2004)

"Never be afraid to try something new. Remember, amateurs built the ark, professionals built the Titanic."
Unknown

"Politeness and consideration for others is like investing pennies and getting dollars back."
Thomas Sowell (1930 –)

"Be polite to all, but intimate with few."
Thomas Jefferson (1743 –1826)

"The secret of success is sincerity. Once you can fake that you've got it made."
Jean Giraudoux (1882 –1944)

9
You Are Not Your Performance

Because most artists recognize that their work will ultimately reflect what's inside their souls, they often confuse ego with execution. Cracking that high C at the end of your song doesn't mean that you're cracked as a person. If you know why you want to sing that high C softly and are prepared to take the risk, then your vision for that note is absolutely virtuous and the only thing missing is a re-evaluation of how you acquire the necessary technique to do it. And yet how often do I hear artists denigrate their entire audition, as well as their entire being, because of a solitary technical blemish? These kinds of irrational self-defeating musings have the potential to destroy self worth and must be stopped. You are not your performance!

An unsuccessful audition does not make you an unsuccessful person. There are a thousand different reasons why you might not have been recalled and most of them are totally out of your control. You might have been too tall, too short; too this or too that – it might have had nothing to do with your performance on the day at all.

OK, let's say your idea of a failed audition is one that didn't go exactly according to your precious master plan. Are you really capable of objectively critiquing your own performance during your audition? If you are, you're clearly not focusing on what you should be – your material! How can you make a judgement about your own audition when you were the participant? You can't and you mustn't!

The world of auditions lies in another dimension. Leave them there in the twilight zone and let the aliens on the audition panel be the judge of their merit. OK, perhaps you do need to improve your discipline a bit; perhaps your technique does require a bit of tweaking. Does that make you some deeply flawed person? Most great artists struggle with their technique and try not to be so lazy – you'll be no different. Nurture who you are, be kind to yourself, focus forwards not back and know that one bad audition doesn't make you one bad person.

"Mistakes are a part of being human. Appreciate your mistakes for what they are: precious life lessons that can only be learned the hard way. Unless it's a fatal mistake, which, at least, others can learn from."

Al Franken (1951 –)"Oh, the Things I Know", 2002

"Avoid having your ego so close to your position that when your position falls, your ego goes with it."

Colin Powell (1937 –)

"I daresay one profits more by the mistakes one makes off one's own bat than by doing the right thing on somebody's else advice."

W. Somerset Maugham (1874 –1965), 'Of Human Bondage', 1915

"Assert your right to make a few mistakes. If people can't accept your imperfections, that's their fault."

Dr. David M. Burns

"Be not ashamed of mistakes and thus make them crimes."

Confucius (551 BC –479 BC)

"When you make a mistake, don't look back at it long. Take the reason of the thing into your mind and then look forward. Mistakes are lessons of wisdom. The past cannot be changed. The future is yet in your power."

Hugh White (1773 –1840)

10
Dress for Success

Although some of my colleagues regularly protest at the complete lack of respect shown by prospective auditionees in how they dress for auditions – ragged dirty jeans or T-shirts saying something like 'Wet' '69' or 'Up Yours' –they express even greater horror when someone walks in wearing a suit and tie. Equally, I'm afraid there does seem to be a rather significant divide between the USA and the UK when it comes to a dress code for auditions. Where American candidates usually come prancing in looking like a peacock, more likely than not their brothers and sisters across the Atlantic lollop onto stage looking like they've just rolled out of the nearest cave.

How does one strike the right balance? Dress neutrally in a way that compliments your shape, without broadcasting its most prominent assets or liabilities. Dress in a way that doesn't scream your sexual persuasion, preferences, or desires. Dress youthfully but within your generation. Dress in a way that makes you feel confident and strong whilst still showing respect for the occasion. Don't run the risk of upstaging what you have on the inside by what you wear on the outside. And remember, first and foremost, we want to see your talent, not your image.

"Keeping your clothes well pressed will keep you from looking hard pressed."
Coleman Cox

"Any piece of clothing can be sexy with a quietly passionate woman inside it."
Anonymous, O Magazine, The Shy Girl's Guide to Sex, Febuary 2003

"Clothes make the man. Naked people have little or no influence on society."

Mark Twain (1835 – 1910)

"Being perfectly well-dressed gives a feeling of tranquility that religion is powerless to bestow."

Ralph Waldo Emerson (1803 –1882), quoting a friend

"In your clothes avoid too much gaudiness; do not value yourself upon an embroidered gown; and remember that a reasonable word, or an obliging look, will gain you more respect than all your fine trappings."

Sir George Savile, 'Advice to a Daughter,' 1688

"The soul of this man is in his clothes."

William Shakespeare (1564 –1616)

If most of us are ashamed of shabby clothes and shoddy furniture, let us be more ashamed of shabby ideas and shoddy philosophies.... It would be a sad situation if the wrapper were better than the meat wrapped inside it.

Albert Einstein (1879-1955)

"People seldom notice old clothes if you wear a big smile."

Lee Mildon

"There is much to support the view that it is clothes that wear us and not we them; we may make them take the mould of arm or breast, but they would mould our hearts, our brains, our tongues to their liking."

Virginia Woolf (1882-1941)

11
Deepen the Well

Whether we like to admit it or not, most of us are slaves to our core beliefs and habitual routines. Unless we consciously make a decision to explore new ways of thinking, feeling, and remembering, most of us will quite happily remain in our little bubbles of, 'I know what I like and I like what I know.' Unless you make a dynamic and determined effort to try new experiences, learn new techniques, break old routines, think the opposite, listen to your instincts, and explore new belief systems, you will never fulfill your potential as an artist.

Take a moment to think about the artists that inspire you and the range and scope of their knowledge and experience. I'm sure that almost without exception, their intellect will be multifaceted and their life experiences will be eclectic and provocative. Even those great artists that work primarily from an intuitive instinct, with perhaps little or no formal training, will have always have really 'lived.'

The more diverse your personal knowledge becomes and the greater the number of new life experiences you grasp, the more chance you'll have at truthfully inhabiting a character which falls outside of your direct experience. Perhaps it's as simple and as profound as having an unquenchable curiosity for life. The more you know, the more you experience, the more you deepen the well. Don't ever let your well run dry!

"The person who has lived the most is not the one with the most years but the one with the richest experiences."

Jean-Jacques Rousseau (1712–1778)

"Life is a series of experiences, each one of which makes us bigger, even though it is hard to realize this. For the world was built to develop character, and we must learn that the setbacks and griefs which we endure help us in our marching onward."

Henry Ford (1863–1947)

"The pain of making the necessary sacrifices always hurts more than you think it's going to. I know. It sucks. That being said, doing something seriously creative is one of the most amazing experiences one can have, in this or any other lifetime. If you can pull it off, it's worth it. Even if you don't end up pulling it off, you'll learn many incredible, magical, valuable things. It's NOT doing it when you know you full well HAD the opportunity- that hurts FAR more than any failure."

Hugh Macleod, How To Be Creative: 12. If you accept the pain, it cannot hurt you., 08-22-04

"The past is finished. There is nothing to be gained by going over it. Whatever it gave us in the experiences it brought us was something we had to know."

Rebecca Beard

"Twenty years from now you will be more disappointed by the things you didn't do than by the ones you did. So throw off the bowlines, sail away from the safe harbor. Catch the trade winds in your sails. Explore. Dream. Discover."

Attributed to Mark Twain (1835-1910)

"I am always doing that which I cannot do, in order that I may learn how to do it."

Pablo Picasso (1881-1973)

12
Play

Even in the times you feel most inspired, trying to get at the truth of a monologue or song is never easy. Sometimes, truth is often revealed to us in the most curious of ways. The more time you allow yourself to experiment or simply play with the material you've chosen, the more individual and unique your version of the truth will become. One of the most enjoyable methods you can use to explore your chosen piece is to play opposites or absurdities. For example, if you're monologue is deadly serious, could you perform it in a way that would make us laugh? If your song is full of anxiety and fear, could you perform it like you don't give a damn? What would your monologue sound like if spoken with a German accent? What if you had to sing your Sondheim song with a Texan drawl? If your song is aggressive and loud, could you sing it softly with vulnerability? What about finding an outrageously flamboyant gesture or pose to suit every individual sentiment in the text? How about peeling an apple or juggling a few tennis balls whilst reciting each verse?

You can expand this idea to individual disciplines as well. If you're a dancer, could you write a poem that would capture the expressiveness of the choreography you must master? If you're a singer, could you create a dance that would reveal the liveliness of rhythm or fluidity of musical line in your song? If you're an actor, could you compose a tune that would accompany and add meaning to your monologue, or perhaps draw a cartoon that encapsulates the core idea of the text?

If any of the above ideas seem childish, good! That's the point. By allowing yourself to simply 'play' you are using all of your imaginative and instinctive faculties to discover the truth of the material as it uniquely and specifically applies to you. By playing opposites or absurdities, you will strengthen your creative powers and reveal hidden possibilities. Play, experiment, gamble and discover your unique truth.

"The Great Man Is He Who Doesn't Lose His Childs heart"

Meneius (503 BC)

"Creativity represents a miraculous coming together of the uninhibited energy of the child with its apparent opposite and enemy, the sense of order imposed on the disciplined adult intelligence."

Norman Podhoretz (1930 –)

"Creativity can solve almost any problem. The creative act, the defeat of habit by originality, overcomes everything."

George Lois (1931 –)

"Humanity has advanced, when it has advanced, not because it has been sober, responsible, and cautious, but because it has been playful, rebellious, and immature."

Tom Robbins (1936 –)

"You can discover more about a person in an hour of play than in a year of conversation."

Plato (427 BC –347 BC)

"The creation of something new is not accomplished by the intellect but by the play instinct acting from inner necessity. The creative mind plays with the objects it loves."

Carl Jung (1875 –1961)

13
Mentors

In Greek mythology, when Odysseus left for the Trojan War he placed the older and wiser Mentor in charge of his palace as well as in charge of his son, Telemachus. This is the origin of the word mentor: a trusted friend or counselor usually in the form of a more experienced person. Mentorship is a concept that has been around for a very long time: Aristotle mentored Alexander the Great, for example. But in modern times, it's the business community in particular that seem to have really embraced the idea of mentorship. Virtually every successful entrepreneur will credit a mentor as having had a significant influence on their success in business, and many CEO's still confer with their mentors.

Having the counsel of someone who's been there, done it, and come out the other side is incredibly useful for anyone who's trying to achieve greater success in their own career. And yet, I'm always amazed at how infrequently artists use this fundamentally simple but fantastically effective concept. Sit down tonight and write out the names of at least three older and more experienced artists you admire. Write a letter to each one simply stating who you are, what you're goals are and why you're asking them to be your mentor. And remember, mentorship can take many different forms: it can be as simple as a ten minute phone call for a bit of advice on how to find the best teacher, personal insight into a particular role or character, a bit of feedback on your last performance at college or procuring a personal reference.

I think you'll be surprised to find that the best artists are usually the most generous and many older, experienced artists will feel privileged to give something back, particularly by offering the benefit of their wisdom to someone who is passionate enough to write to them personally and ask for their help.

The old adage of 'It's not what you know, but whom you know,' doesn't have to be viewed cynically. In fact, I think the phrase should more accurately read,

'Who you know will determine what you know.' Find a mentor, be respectful of their wisdom, and you will benefit immeasurably.

"Successful people turn everyone who can help them into sometime mentors!"
John Crosby (1859 – 1943)

"Mentor: Someone whose hindsight can become your foresight."
Anonymous

"He who wrestles with us strengthens our nerves and sharpens our skill. Our antagonist is our helper."
Edmund Burke (1729 –1797)

"The best advisers, helpers and friends, always are not those who tell us how to act in special cases, but who give us, out of themselves, the ardent spirit and desire to act right, and leave us then, even through many blunders, to find out what our own form of right action is."
Phillips Brooks (1835 –1893)

"In the multitude of counselors there is safety."
Bible, Proverbs xi.

14
Senses

Sometimes when I watch outstanding auditions, I feel so privileged to witness how a skilful artist can utilize every part of their body and intellect to create a performance that is so seamless and whole. Touch, taste, sight, smell, hearing, intellect and soul all come together to create something quite greater than the sum of its parts – it's the mystery and mastery of theatre performance and it can only be achieved when each sense connects and vibrates synchronously with all the others.

If you're singing a love song, can you smell her perfume? If your monologue is written in verse, can you feel its rhythm course through your veins? If your dance is lyrical, is your body singing? By searching for and engaging all of your senses you'll be able to experience and communicate in ways that might not have initially been self-evident.

Regardless of how intelligently you turn a phrase, unless you really taste the flavour and touch the meaning of each word, no one will ever really believe you. No matter how beautifully you execute that devlopé, unless you see and hear why it must be beautiful, no one will care very much. In spite of how powerfully you sing that high belt note, unless your whole body screams out the reason for doing so, its musical energy will be vacuous.

Ultimately, the integrity or your auditions will be determined by your ability to use and unify each of your senses. If you look, listen, smell, touch, taste and yearn for understanding, your whole body will resonate with the story you want to tell.

"I want all my senses engaged. Let me absorb the world's variety and uniqueness."
Maya Angelou (1928 –)

"Our five senses are incomplete without the sixth —a sense of humor."
Author Unknown

"Nothing can cure the soul but the senses, just as nothing can cure the senses but the soul."
Oscar Wilde (1854 –1900), The Picture of Dorian Gray

"All credibility, all good conscience, all evidence of truth come only from the senses."
Friedrich Nietzsche (1844 –1900)

"When the five senses and the mind are still, and the reasoning intellect rests in silence, then begins the highest path. This calm steadiness of the senses is called yoga. Then one should become watchful, because yoga comes and goes."
Katha Upanishad

"If any thing is sacred the human body is sacred."
Walt Whitman (1819 –1892)

"But all art is sensual and poetry particularly so. It is directly, that is, of the senses, and since the senses do not exist without an object for their employment all art is necessarily objective. It doesn't declaim or explain, it presents."
William Carlos Williams (1883 – 1963)

15
Hit the Ball Back

One of the most difficult techniques an actor must master, both in an audition and on stage, is to respond to what you actually receive rather than to what you have preconceived. Another way of putting it might be to say you must hit the ball back in a way that takes into consideration the spin, pace and purpose of the approaching shot.

John McEnroe is a great example of someone who was a master at reading each of his opponent's shots with an almost preternatural acuteness and instinctiveness. In a blink of an eye, he would be able to respond and hit the ball back with an authoritative and intuitive genius. This is something that only came from years of a very special kind of concentration – a concentration that dealt purely with what he was given at any moment in time within a match. McEnroe would take the most blistering of serves and hit the ball back with a subtle backspin at a fraction of the pace, obliterating his opponent's offensive game. Did he consciously make the decision how to return that serve before he received it? Of course not. His years of training to focus solely on the incoming ball rather than any preconceived return enabled his instincts to take over and respond effortlessly in a fraction of a second.

It's important to remember that taking an audition is ultimately a spontaneous and intuitive event. Preparation and practice improve your artistry, increase your confidence and enhance your chances of success, but ultimately anything can happen in that room and on that stage. Try not to script a response to every eventuality and embrace the excitement of knowing that you can't possibly anticipate everything that will occur. Focus solely on what you are given and you will find yourself open and able to hit the ball back with as much variation and spontaneous genius as John McEnroe.

"As long as we respond predictably to what feels good and what feels bad, it is easy for others to exploit our preferences for their own ends."

Mihaly Csikszentmihalyi (1934 –) Flow: The Psychology of Optimal Experience, 1990

"What we anticipate seldom occurs; what we least expected generally happens."

Benjamin Disraeli (1804 –1881)

"We want the facts to fit the preconceptions. When they don't, it is easier to ignore the facts than to change the preconceptions."

Jessamyn West (1902 –1984)

"We are always getting ready to live but never living."

Ralph Waldo Emerson (1803 – 1882)

"We have two ears and one mouth so that we can listen twice as much as we speak"

Epictetus (ca.55-ca.135)

"The most important thing in communication is to hear what isn't being said."

Peter F. Drucker (1909-2005)

"Things turn out best for the people who make the best out of the way things turn out."

Art Linkletter (1912-)

"A successful person is one who can lay a firm foundation with the bricks that others throw at him or her."

David Brinkley (1920-2003)

16
Where to Focus?

The problem of where to direct your focus in an audition is an age-old dilemma, and one that elicits a multitude of different opinions. Recommendations like, 'Direct your focus three feet above the heads of the audition panel' or, 'imagine you are on stage and the audition panel is your audience' seem terribly pedantic and actually beside the point.

Whatever material you've chosen for your audition has a context. It is, or is part of, a dramatic scene. Your duty as an actor, first and foremost, is to immerse yourself completely in that scene and bring that moment to life, regardless of whether it's in an audition, rehearsal or live performance. By concentrating on content and context your external focus will be right because it will simply be natural to the scene. If you accomplish only this one thing for your auditions, you'll be heads and shoulders more interesting than the vast majority of auditionees who strike some generalized pose and focus in some generic way.

Of course there are certain practicalities to acknowledge –the audition panel need to see and hear you clearly for instance. But ultimately, we want to see you give an audition that realizes the underlining truth of the material you've chosen. That's how we'll understand what kind of actor you are; that's how you'll best reveal the talents you have inside of you. Arguments like, 'should I look directly at members of the audition panel' become inconsequential because you're properly focusing on being an artist, rather than giving some sort of codified impression of a performance.

On a side note, remember that in all likelihood your focus will be interrupted by any number of distractions emanating from the audition panel. It is crucial that you mentally prepare yourself to accept that whatever you're giving might not be received in the way you'd like. An audition panel is there to do a job –we may need to confer, jot down evaluations, read your CV, or exchange notes or papers.

One member may be shaking their head, another may be chuckling. None of it should concern you. There's nothing insidious about it —remember, you're the one performing. We're there to do a different kind of job altogether —it's just business. Whatever distractions come from the table do not warrant any notice from you – it would be a great shame if you ended up focusing on our evaluation and response to your audition rather than the audition itself.

Keep it simple and clear; find your space, realize the scene and carpe diem!

"The best audience is intelligent, well-educated, and a little drunk."
Alben W. Barkley (1877 – 1956) (vice president under Harry Truman)

"A mind troubled by doubt cannot focus on the course to victory."
Arthur Golden (1956 –), Memoirs of a Geisha, 1997

"In Kyudo philosophy, you don't aim--you become one with the target. Then, in fact, there's nothing to aim at. I find it works well with women, too. Give it a try."
Martin Sage and Sybil Adelman, Northern Exposure, The Bumpy Road to Love, 1991

"I'm a word man. See, there's this theory about the nature of tragedy, that Aristotle didn't mean catharsis for the audience but a purgation of emotions for the actors themselves. The audience is just a witness to the event taking place on stage."
Jim Morrison (1943 – 1971)

17
Double, Double Toil and Trouble!

Double, double toil and trouble; Fire burn, and caldron bubble!

Auditions often feel so frightening that we'd quite willingly boil up eye of newt, toe of frog, wool of bat, and tongue of dog if only to stop our knees knocking and our hands shaking. Sometimes auditions loom so menacingly in our imaginations that you've got to find new and creative ways to demystify the entire process. Putting the shoe on the other foot and finding out what it's like from our perspective, on the other side of the audition table, is one of the best ways I know to melt away the witches of self-doubt in your head.

Ask your former tutor at Drama College if you can assist them at their next round of auditions for new students. Workshop your own production, which you cast and direct yourself. Create an audition guild where all members must alternate between sitting on the panel and auditioning themselves. Ask a resident creative team member on a local production if you could observe a day's auditioning. Take on a group of private pupils and help them prepare for their own auditions.

Once you begin to widen your frame of reference, you'll instinctively adopt a more objective and cool-headed view about auditioning and learn to relax. By shifting your perspective away from yourself and learning to empathize with the poor bastards that sit on audition panels, you'll shed the psychological weight of auditioning whilst gaining a priceless view of the good, bad and ugly of audition behavior and technique. Don't give auditions any more credit than they're due. At the end of the day they're merely a means to an end. Expand your view and look at the big picture and you'll find that you can finally silence the audition witches in your head!

"Could we change our attitude, we should not only see life differently, but life itself would come to be different. Life would undergo a change of appearance because we ourselves had undergone a change in attitude."

Katherine Mansfield (1888 –1923)

"Any fact facing us is not as important as our attitude toward it, for that determines our success or failure. The way you think about a fact may defeat you before you ever do anything about it. You are overcome by the fact because you think you are."

Norman Vincent Peale (1898 –1993)

"The great gift of human beings is that we have the power of empathy."

Meryl Streep (1949 –)

"I happen to feel that the degree of a person's intelligence is directly reflected by the number of conflicting attitudes she can bring to bear on the same topic."

Lisa Alther (1944 –) Kinflicks, 1975

"And there was a beautiful view

But nobody could see.

Cause everybody on the island

Was saying: Look at me! Look at me!"

Laurie Anderson (1947 –) Language Is A Virus

18
Enthusiasm

Enthusiasm is probably the most powerful single attitude an actor can call upon when taking an audition. Genuine enthusiasm not only has the magical ability to quell most audition judders, it is also one of the most important professional characteristics an audition panel will look for in casting their production. Enthusiasm is a quality that affects everything else you do. When an actor is enthusiastic, they listen and respond better, they relax and perform more freely, and their capacity to concentrate and focus on the dramatic impetus of material is greatly enhanced.

I'm not suggesting for one moment you parade your enthusiasm before the audition panel like some self satisfied peacock; that would only tell volumes about your enthusiasm for how you're being perceived. Enthusiasm is simply a spirited commitment, a strong sense of a responsibility to be faithful to your material, and an optimistic attitude.

But perhaps the most important aspects of enthusiasm aren't really quantifiable. We all know that we simply like to be in the presence of enthusiastic people –we all like to have enthusiastic friends, family, and colleagues. I think we are all instinctively drawn to positive energy and enthusiasm generates bucket loads of it. Working with enthusiastic colleagues make the days go faster and the work go smoother. Enthusiasm is terribly infectious and enthusiastic work mates help us dive into our own work with joie de vivre!

If you think about it, enthusiastic people quite simply send out all the right signals to potential employers: good work ethic, being unselfish, sense of fun, being a good listener, hopeful, trusting and optimistic. Every director recognizes how crucially important it is to have enthusiasm in your cast, not just for opening night but more importantly when show number 500 comes around.

And when all else fails, sometimes genuine enthusiasm will save you from yourself. I've seen some of the most appalling auditions where every conceivable thing that could go wrong did, and yet the actor was given a call back simply because their sense of enthusiasm was so utterly attractive. Don't forget, there isn't an enthusiasm gene. It's a conscious choice to shift your energy from blasé to exuberant, nonchalant to passionate. Make the choice! Make the shift and see the results!

"If you aren't fired with enthusiasm, you will be fired with enthusiasm."
Vince Lombardi (1913 –1970)

"You will do foolish things, but do them with enthusiasm."
Colette (1873 –1954), in New York World-Telegram and Sun, 1961

"Nothing great was ever achieved without enthusiasm."
Ralph Waldo Emerson (1803 –1882)

"Think enthusiastically about everything; but especially about your job. If you do, you'll put a touch of glory in your life. If you love your job with enthusiasm, you'll shake it to pieces. You'll love it into greatness."
Norman Vincent Peale (1898 –1993)

"Every great and commanding moment in the annals of the world is the triumph of some enthusiasm."
Ralph Waldo Emerson (1803 –1882)

19
Surf the Wave

Every song or monologue has an internal ebb and flow that is undeniable and waiting to be discovered. Find the power and velocity of that dramatic wave and surf it! How dull life would be if every song lyric were delivered dead in time or every punctuation mark religiously adhered to. I don't suggest for a second you use variation as an end unto itself but merely point out that musical notation and punctuation are guides or maps for the artist to use to enhance their own understanding of the text and help guide their interpretation, so that they may better express the intended meaning of the composer, lyricist or author.

Each melody, each lyric, each bit of verse or prose will resonate differently for every person. What makes you uniquely individual in intellect, imagination, physique and experience will determine how you surf that particular artistic wave. Will you misinterpret the undercurrents and miss the wave altogether? Or will you bring your wit, rhythm and intuition together to find that perfect moment where you can cascade down the front wall of that wave using its power to inspire your own dance upon it? The sea can be unforgiving and so can art. Continuous back phrasing, pregnant pauses, rushing ahead, ignoring breaths, forgetting commas, waiting forever after full stops can all deny the internal rhythm of a good song or monologue. Find its internal rhythm, find its momentum, find where it needs to breathe and you'll be able to surf the wave.

"Self-trust is the essence of heroism."

Ralph Waldo Emerson (1803 –1882)

"There is in us a lyric germ or nucleus which deserves respect; it bids a man to ponder or create; and in this dim corner of himself he can take refuge and find consolations which the society of his fellow creatures does not provide."

Norman Douglas (1868 – 1952)

"Challenges are gifts that force us to search for a new center of gravity. Don't fight them. Just find a different way to stand."

Oprah Winfrey (1954 –), O Magazine, October 2002

"I want to stay as close to the edge as I can without going over. Out on the edge you see all kinds of things you can't see from the center."

Kurt Vonnegut (1922 –2007)

"One doesn't discover new lands without consenting to lose sight of the shore for a very long time."

Andre Gide (1868 – 1951)

"I have a simple philosophy: Fill what's empty. Empty what's full. Scratch where it itches."

Alice Roosevelt Longworth (1884-1980)

"Following straight lines shortens distances, and also life."

Antonio Porchia (1885-1968) Voces, 1943, translated from Spanish by W.S. Merwin

"Why not go out on a limb? Isn't that where the fruit is?"

Frank Scully (1892 – 1964)

20
Stand On Your Head

Most of us are slaves to habit. We repeat the same processes day in and day out and hope that our consistency of effort and the habits we've formed will eventually reap the rewards we want. But what should we do when our habits don't lead to success and don't reap the rewards we desire? The unfortunate fact is that most of us simply embrace our habits with even more conviction and steadfastness rather than venture into unknown experiences. Albert Einstein once said that the definition of insanity is doing the same thing over and over expecting different results. Repetition without focus and imaginative thought is the kiss of death for artists.

Is your audition song feeling tired? LEARN A NEW ONE! Is your audition monologue boring you? IMAGINE WHAT IT'S DOING TO THE PANEL! Does your voice lack power and resonance? LEARN A NEW WAY TO BREATHE! . Do you tend to forget your words on the day? PRACTICE THEM STANDING ON YOUR HEAD! If it's song, speak it. If it's dialogue, sing it. If it's poetry, dance it!

Creativity and the willingness to embrace change are the most important combatants of habit. Unless you consciously and regularly step into the void of the unknown, your habits will end up determining your potential instead of your imagination unlocking your future. Practice Invention! Invention will open up insights you couldn't possibly have imagined within the comfort of your gilded box of habits. Step out of the box, engage your imagination and rediscover the joy of new experiences.

"I passionately hate the idea of being with it, I think an artist has always to be out of step with his time."

Orson Welles (1915 –1985)

"In human life, art may arise from almost any activity, and once it does so, it is launched on a long road of exploration, invention, freedom to the limits of extravagance, interference to the point of frustration, finally discipline, controlling constant change and growth."

Susanne Langer (1895 –1985)

"If life doesn't offer a game worth playing, then invent a new one."

Anthony J. D'Angelo (1972 -), The College Blue Book, 1995

"Would I had phrases that are not known, utterances that are strange, in new language that has not been used, free from repetition, not an utterance which has grown stale, which men of old have spoken."

Egyptian Inscription Recorded at the Time of the Invention of Writing

"When you are through changing, you are through."

Bruce Barton (1886-1967)

"Change always comes bearing gifts."

Price Pritchett

"The only difference between a rut and a grave is their dimensions."

Ellen Glasgow (1873-1945)

"Habit, if not resisted, soon becomes necessity."

St. Augustine (354-430)

21
Analysis Leads to Paralysis

When preparing to take any audition, it is incredibly important that you do as much research as you can about the production for which you are auditioning, that you choose appropriate material to prepare, that you understand and determine how you're going to express that material, and that you practice, practice and practice, hoping on the day you don't forget text or tune. Within that process, it's terribly easy for any actor to become paralyzed with anxiety, fear or nervousness by over-contemplating or analyzing what they are about to do. Questions like 'How should I?' and 'What if?' take you further and further away from the purpose of your audition: to reveal to the panel the passion in your soul and the intelligence of your thoughts.

Remember that when the time comes for you to start that song or monologue, it is not the time for you to be thinking about the 'position of your larynx' or 'does my bum look big in this dress?' The less you think about yourself and the more you think about the material you've chosen the better. Focus, like an arrow speeding through the air to the centre of its target, on expressing those words and that melody with a genuine and open heart. Know that in that instant, everything else is outside your control and that ultimately all the audition panel wants to understand is your fervour, your zeal for being an artist. Phrases like 'Carpe Diem,' 'Just Do It,' and 'Go for It' should become your audition mantra. Most importantly, remember that like everything else, the feeling of letting go and focusing on the flow of your intuitive passion and expressiveness must be practiced not just at the audition, but also in the rehearsal room.

"It is only by following your deepest instinct that you can lead a rich life, and if you let your fear of consequences prevent you from following your deepest instinct, then your life will be safe, expedient and thin."

Katharine Butler Hathaway (1890 – 1942)

"There can be as much value in the blink of an eye as in months of rational analysis."

Malcolm Gladwell (1963 –)

Blink: The Power of Thinking Without Thinking, 2005

"Art is collaboration between God and the artist, and the less the artist does the better."

Andre Gidé (1869 – 1951)

"Truth is subject to too much analysis."

Frank Herbert (1920 – 1986), Dune, 1965

"Half of analysis is anal."

Marty Indik

"All great men are gifted with intuition. They know without reasoning or analysis, what they need to know."

Alexis Carrel (1873 –1944)

"Reasoning at every step he treads, Man yet mistakes his way, Whilst meaner things, whom instinct leads, Are rarely known to stray."

William Cowper (1731-1800)

"The most decisive actions of our life... are most often unconsidered actions."

André Gide (1869 – 1951), The Counterfeiters, 1926

22
Repetition

When we repeat a thought or physical action often enough, it eventually becomes a habit and when our habits are then reinforced through further repetitions, they in turn become automatic reflexes. This is an extremely important process to understand because used well, it can make all the difference to your career; used poorly and it could possibly destroy you.

Every time you rehearse in a calm and thoughtful manner, you are reinforcing what it feels like to perform in a relaxed and intelligent way. Every time you practice your song in an anxious or distracted state, you are solidifying behaviour and technique that will ultimately be counterproductive.

Each time you consciously visualize what was most successful about how you performed in your most recent audition, you are strengthening your body's ability to repeat and improve upon that same positive performance. Each time you pick through your latest audition performance with the fine toothcomb of self-criticism, you are weakening your body's ability to produce under pressure.

Whatever behaviour you repeat time and time again will eventually become a habit, whether it's a negative or positive visualization, a stressful or relaxed technique or an unfocused or focused performance. Once those habits are reinforced through further repetition, they become absolutely automatic and ingrained. This is why it is so critical that when you repeat anything, you do it with serenity, self-possession and intelligence.

You will achieve far more with three 20-minute sessions of focused practice spread out over the day than hours of repetition when distracted or angry. When you practice in a stressful state, you are creating bad habits which are incredibly resilient to change and will take Herculean efforts to repair. The idea that practice makes perfect only holds up in the most ideal circumstances. What practice most definitely will do is reinforce whatever state of mind, method, mode or technique you are using whilst carrying out the repetition, and it will do it to such an extent that it eventually becomes absolute instinct. How sad it would be if every time you go for that high C your instinct were to constrict and muscle it out. It doesn't have to be that way. Train smart and repeat astutely. Only then will you stand a chance at your practice making perfect.

"The person with a fixed goal, a clear picture of his desire, or an ideal always before him, causes it, through repetition, to be buried deeply in his subconscious mind and is thus enabled, thanks to its generative and sustaining power, to realize his goal in a minimum of time and with a minimum of physical effort. Just pursue the thought unceasingly. Step by step you will achieve realization, for all your faculties and powers become directed to that end."
Claude M. Bristol (1891 – 1951)

"Some people say that practice makes perfect but I just feel that the repetition works against me and I start thinking too far ahead during a show."
Rick Savage (1960 –)

"Any ideas, plan, or purpose may be placed in the mind through repetition of thought."
Napoleon Hill (1883 – 1970)

"The happiness of most people we know is not ruined by great catastrophes or fatal errors, but by the repetition of slowly destructive little things."
Ernest Dimnet (1866 – 1954)

"We cannot always control our thoughts, but we can control our words, and repetition impresses the subconscious, and we are then master of the situation."
Florence Scovel Shinn (1802 – 1866)

23
Stand Tall

Fear can affect our bodies in the most extraordinary ways especially in auditions. I've seen eyelids quiver in exact time with an actor's vibrato. I've seen legs shake in 12/8 when the music was in 3/4. I've seen hunched shoulders, bowed backs, and nervous feet. I've seen unblinking eyes dart back and forth furiously looking for a way to escape, like Alex being tortured in Clockwork Orange. I've seen arms frozen and stiff hanging like two planks of wood hinged on to arm sockets. I've seen grown men faint and grown women vomit. Fear can affect our physiology in a thousand different ways and I don't for one second mean to index each of these manifestations flippantly. They are not funny when they're happening to you. But it does stand to reason that if fear can affect our physicality, then our physicality should be able to affect our level of fear.

First and foremost, stand tall. Stand like the Empire State Building. Stand like you have as much right as anyone else to be there, because you do. Don't be caught sitting inertly in an uncomfortable chair with your head in hands when your name is called. Make sure your body is awake, vibrant, alive and in motion. Stretch, breathe, find your own little corner where you can do what you need to do to stay physically loose and relaxed. When your name is called, stand up straight and embrace the adventure. Stand like a prince or a warrior. Stand like Laurence Olivier or Grace Kelly. Let the strength of your backbone drive out the fear. And smile! Not for us, but because you have the guts to walk straight into your fear and grasp the challenge —standing tall all the while!

"The body is a marvelous machine...a chemical laboratory, a power-house. Every movement, voluntary or involuntary, full of secrets and marvels!"

Theodor Herzl (1860 –1904)

"The simple solution for disappointing depression: Get up and get moving. Physically move. Do. Act. Get going."

Peter McWilliams (1949 – 2000), Life 101, 1994

"Our own physical body possesses a wisdom which we who inhabit the body lack."

Henry Miller (1891 – 1980)

"You can stand tall, without standing on someone. You can be a victor without having victims."

Harriet Woods (1927 – 2007)

"Help others get ahead. You will always stand taller with someone else on your shoulders."

Bob Moawad (1941 – 2007)

"Emotion always has its roots in the unconscious and manifests itself in the body."

Irene Claremont de Castillejo (1885 – 1967)

"Man is an intelligence in servitude to his organs."

Aldous Huxley (1894 – 1963)

"A trembling in the bones may carry a more convincing testimony than the dry documented deductions of the brain."

Llewellyn Powers (1836 – 1908)

24
Respect Reaps Results

Quite apart from the fact that self-respect and respect for others are simply good humanistic values, they also have a practical value which can be magnified tenfold when you are seeking employment. From the moment you step through the door of the address you've been given for your audition, you must assume that everyone you encounter has a connection, and that one connection is not more important than another. I've seen many an audition change course for the worse after the stage manager revealed to the director how rudely they've just been treated by the last candidate. For all you know, the stage-door man may be the choreographer's boyfriend –do you really want to run the risk of taking out your frustrations on him just because you had the journey from hell on your way to the audition? I've seen candidates virtually discounted on the spot when they've displayed their frustration at the audition pianist for not keeping up. Oops, the pianist turned out to be the Music Director.

If you are charm personified to the director and Regan (from the Exorcist) to the company manager, you're walking on very thin ice indeed. In terms of seeking employment, almost no other quality is detested more than duplicity of character. It suggests deviousness, a general lack of integrity, and most importantly, a total absence of respect.

I'm a great believer that we reap what we sow and therefore respect and honesty in your personal life are vitally important to achieve success in your professional life. Some might argue that everything artists do on stage is, by its very nature, duplicitous. I don't subscribe to that idea at all. I believe that your auditions and stage performances are ultimately a distillation of your greater nature. Your truthfulness and good character in your personal life will ultimately determine your ability to be truthful and of good character as an actor. This is precisely why actors feel so vulnerable in auditions –they instinctively know this to be true.

That's not to say that if you are Regan, you won't do well in auditions. Quite the contrary, there is lots of room for demonically possessed actors in theatre, and you'll no doubt make fools of many a director. But respect for yourself, respect for your colleagues, respect for your craft and respect for auditions will go a long way toward making you a better person, as well as a more successful actor.

"He that respects himself is safe from others. He wears a coat of mail that none can pierce."

Henry Wadsworth Longfellow (1807 – 1882)

"Respect a man, he will do the more."

James Howell (1594 – 1666)

"We confide in our strength, without boasting of it; we respect that of others, without fearing it."

Thomas Jefferson (1743 – 1826)

"For to be free is not merely to cast off one's chains, but to live in a way that respects and enhances the freedom of others."

Nelson Mandela (1918 –)

"The capacity for getting along with our neighbor depends to a large extent on the capacity for getting along with ourselves. The self-respecting individual will try to be as tolerant of his neighbor's shortcomings as he is of his own."

Eric Hoffer (1902 – 1983)

"There is no respect for others without humility in one's self."

Henri Frederic Amiel (1821 – 1881)

25
Don't Lie

This may seem like the most obvious piece of advice, but it warrants a mention simply because lying is something we encounter all the time and it quite simply pisses us off. Many CVs are simply works of fiction. Can I say once and for all that being an understudy is not the same as playing the role. Taking a master class or two does not give you the right to claim you have a degree. 'Strong dancer' means you can learn difficult choreography quickly, not that you can put one foot in front of the other in time to music. If you're close to getting your free senior bus pass, why does your CV still read 39 years of age? If your shape is that of a watermelon, don't claim you look like a banana. If your experience is nil, fabrication will not make you magically a more interesting prospect to us. Lying always carries with it the potential to backfire in the most ghastly ways. Don't do it!

Not lying isn't just about the accuracy of your CV. It can be as simple as you saying you understand when you don't. When a director goes into a complex explanation of what he or she wants from you as an actor, feigning understanding and not delivering can be so much more harmful than simply asking for further clarification. At least then you stand a chance at being able to give them what they want. Think about it. How often are we able to pick up and detect when we're being lied to? In an audition situation, most lies are incredibly transparent and if they're not, they're incredibly easy for us to test. Would you want to hire a liar? Nor will we. Don't do it, ever!

"He who is not very strong in memory should not meddle with lying."
Michel de Montaigne (1533 – 1592)

"I was not lying. I said things that later on seemed to be untrue."
Richard Nixon (1913 – 1994) discussing Watergate

"Too many people confine their exercise to jumping to conclusions, running up bills, stretching the truth, bending over backward, lying down on the job, sidestepping responsibility and pushing their luck."
Author Unknown

"The lip of truth shall be established forever: but a lying tongue is but for a moment."
Proverbs 12:19, The King James Bible

"There are three kinds of lies: lies, damned lies, and statistics."
Benjamin Disraeli (1804 – 1881)

"Truth fears no questions."
Unknown

"If you do not tell the truth about yourself you cannot tell it about other people"
Virginia Woolfe (1882 – 1941)

"Oh what a tangled web we weave, When first we practise to deceive"
Sir Walter Scott (1771 – 1832)

26
Baby Steps

'What About Bob' is a very funny film about a multiphobic, obsessive compulsive psychiatric patient, played by Bill Murray, who only gains the strength to face the outside world after reading his psychiatrist's best selling book, 'Baby Steps.' Bill Murray's character learns to conquer his phobias by setting small achievable targets and building confidence as each one is completed. By celebrating a succession of many small victories, he finally regains his self-respect but unfortunately drives his psychiatrist completely insane in the process.

Sometimes the best lessons are taught from the funniest teachers, and learning how to celebrate small victories like Bill Murray in Baby Steps is no bad idea when it comes to building up your self-esteem for auditions. Singing your song without your lip quivering, taking in big proper breaths before each phrase, being composed enough to respond intelligently and spontaneously to a question, singing that last note perfectly in tune or perhaps just showing up to the damn audition in the first place are all small achievable targets worthy of being celebrated when you complete them! Set the goal posts so you can win! Your confidence will thank you.

So often we make the mistake of measuring success or failure solely by end results. 'I didn't win the audition therefore I must be a failure!' If you measure your success as an actor solely on your track record of auditions won, you've just rigged the entire game against yourself. Athletes become champions by measuring their success on an upward progression of personal bests, and not whether they win every race they enter. As an auditioning actor, it's crucial you find more productive ways of measuring success than just 'win or lose.' Learn to take baby steps. Learn to celebrate even your smallest victories and you'll eventually learn how to win!

"The key to realizing a dream is to focus not on success but significance —and then even the small steps and little victories along your path will take on greater meaning."

Oprah Winfrey (1954 –), O Magazine, September

"I have never been especially impressed by the heroics of people who are convinced they are about to change the world. I am more awed by those who struggle to make one small difference after another."

Ellen Goodman (1941 –)

"Character is forged in the smallest of struggles. Then, when the big challenges come, we're ready."

Waiter Rant, Waiter Rant weblog, 12-30-05

"Nothing is too small to know, and nothing is too big to attempt."

William Van Horne (1843 – 1915)

It is not growing like a tree

In bulk doth make man better be;

Or standing long an oak, three hundred year,

To fall a log at last, dry, bald, and sere:

A lily of a day

Is fairer far in May,

Although it fall and die that night –

It was the plant and flower of light.

In small proportions we just beauties see;

And in short measures life may perfect be.

Benjamin Jonson (1572 – 1637)

27
Peace

Sometimes the most important thing you can do as an artist is to take the phone off the hook and have a bath. Listen to a symphony or walk in the woods. Lie on your back and concentrate on nothing more than your breathing. Go horseback riding or skydiving. Ride your bike until you can't pedal any more. Take a long sauna. Accept only one deadline this week and say 'no' to at least three things that demand your time. Make love all morning long and follow with a slow late breakfast. Have a massage. Listen to Glenn Gould playing Bach. Paint a watercolour. Draw a cartoon. Read a silly book. Be still!

It's so important to switch off the white noise of our lives in order to switch back on in High Definition. When was the last time you simply gave yourself the space and opportunity to just observe life? When was the last time you took 15 minutes out of your day to meditate? When was the last time you broke your routine and learned something completely new? Recharging your creative batteries is a must if you are to succeed as an actor. Being creative by its very nature requires the time to wander, drift and experiment. So many actors I know are so ambitious and driven that the speed at which they travel through each day means most of life passes them by. Be quiet for a time. Breathe deeply. For your next audition, show up an hour early, find a space and stretch, breathe and meditate rather than frantically rushing at the last minute to make your appointed time. Think Peace instead of Pace and you'll find that success will flow your way.

"The problem is never how to get new, innovative thoughts into your mind, but how to get old ones out. Every mind is a building filled with archaic furniture. Clean out a corner of your mind and creativity will instantly fill it."

Dee Hock (1929 –)

"Creativity is allowing yourself to make mistakes. Art is knowing which ones to keep."

Scott Adams (1957 –)

"Don't think. Thinking is the enemy of creativity. It's self-conscious, and anything self-conscious is lousy. You can't try to do things. You simply must do things."

Ray Bradbury (1920 –)

"In the attitude of silence the soul finds the path in a clearer light, and what is elusive and deceptive resolves itself into crystal clearness. Our life is a long and arduous quest after Truth."

Mahatma Gandhi (1869 –1948)

"There are some things you learn best in calm, and some in storm."

Willa Cather (1873 –1947), The Song of the Lark, 1915

"I love people. I love my family, my children…but inside myself is a place where I live all alone and that's where you renew your springs that never dry up."

Pearl S Buck (1892-1973)

"To live content with small means; to seek elegance rather than luxury, and refinement rather than fashion; to be worthy, not respectable, and wealthy, not rich; to listen to stars and birds, babes and sages, with open heart; to study hard; to think quietly, act frankly, talk gently, await occasions, hurry never; in a word, to let the spiritual, unbidden and unconscious, grow up through the common--this is my symphony."

William Henry Channing (1810-1884)

28
Showing Up Is Half the Battle

Can you think of a reason why you'd cancel a dental appointment to have a tooth pulled or not show up to your proctologist examination? I can think of a hundred reasons, but the amazing thing is that most of us **do** show up for the tooth-pulling ordeal; we won't cancel the rectal examination because we know it's best for us in the long term, even though it might be painful in the short term. Although some actors may argue that having a tooth pulled or their prostate prodded would be less painful than an audition, it's important to remember the phrase, 'short term pain for long term gain.' In other words, show up and you're half way there!

Every agent I know has what I call a SNSC or Serial No Show Client. Let me give you a brief but typical example. Agent Mike calls client Sam; they discuss details of the audition ad naseum; agent Mike confirms time with said producer; Sam never turns up.

Occasionally, actors will call with absolutely fantastic excuses, but most of the time it's simply a NS with a NRG: No Show with a No Reason Given. And if I see their name on my list audition after audition and have never actually had the pleasure of meeting them, they are then elevated to the status of a SNSC.

The SNSC has such an intense short-term fear that he or she will simply not show up to the audition and as a result, forfeit any potential long-term gain. It just goes to prove that our internal demons are far more potent and dangerous than any external threat we may face. SNSC's are just too scared to give themselves a chance at enjoying a brighter future.

In the United Kingdom, the National Lottery has a marketing slogan that reads, 'You can't win it if you're not in it.' I've decided to start a joint campaign with all theatrical agents to ensure that this slogan is printed in giant red type across the top of all their agent/client contracts. For all you SNSC's out there, auditions do not cause physical pain. They do not make the world stop revolving. They are insignificant events which will become easier and easier the more of them you attend. Some actors find they actually begin to enjoy auditions and occasionally learn something new for free. Go! Be brave! Show up! Remember auditions can't possibly hurt as much as having your prostate prodded.

"Few men are willing to brave the disapproval of their fellows, the censure of their colleagues, the wrath of their society. Moral courage is a rarer commodity than bravery in battle or great intelligence. Yet it is the one essential, vital quality for those who seek to change a world which yields most painfully to change."
Robert F. Kennedy (1925 –1968), 1966 speech

"Courage is the art of being the only one who knows you're scared to death."
Harold Wilson (1916 –1995)

"Courage and perseverance have a magical talisman, before which difficulties disappear and obstacles vanish into air."
John Quincy Adams (1767 –1848)

"Life shrinks or expands in proportion to one's courage."
Anais Nin (1903 –1977), The Diary of Anais Nin, volume 3, 1939-1944

"Seventy percent of success in life is showing up."
Woody Allen (1935-)

29
Teachers

One of the wondrous aspects of being an artist is that the deeper you probe and investigate your craft, the more you realize there is to learn. The process of developing your art is boundless; there is no endgame, no finish, no completion. But one thing all artists who continually strive to achieve greater heights have in common is the utilization and employment of master teachers. Whatever point you have reached in your artistic journey, make the investment in time and money to seek out and use the very best teachers you can find.

You can learn more from one lesson with a master than you can from years of work with a wannabe. In fact, more damage comes from not employing the very best than you might know. Don't make that mistake – you'd be far better off with your own imagination, intuition, and passion than with some mediocrity of a teacher!

Of course you must ultimately follow your own instincts in your search for the right teacher, but don't allow yourself to ignore the fact that all good teachers will possess certain fundamental criteria. First and foremost, a teacher is someone who is passionate and obsessive about their subject. A teacher is someone who is constantly learning themselves. A teacher is someone who has an infectious curiosity about all aspects of their art. A teacher is someone who understands the courage required to take an audition, the discipline demanded to cultivate a good technique and the mystery and art in giving a great performance. A teacher is someone who will work with each student in an entirely unique way, recognizing and respecting the individuality and originality of each student. A teacher will continually challenge you and ask the tough questions. A teacher will help you find methods to relax and make your art look effortless. Finally, a teacher will be a master themselves, perhaps not in the same discipline as you, but a master nonetheless. Search for such teachers and once you find them, cherish and use them all your life.

"An understanding heart is everything in a teacher, and cannot be esteemed highly enough. One looks back with appreciation to the brilliant teachers, but with gratitude to those who touched our human feeling. The curriculum is so much necessary raw material, but warmth is the vital element for the growing plant and for the soul of the child."

Carl Jung (1875 –1961)

"Teachers open the door. You enter by yourself."

Chinese Proverb

"The true teacher defends his pupils against his own personal influence."

Amos Bronson Alcott (1799 –1888)

"The best teacher is the one who suggests rather than dogmatizes, and inspires his listener with the wish to teach himself."

Edward Bulwer-Lytton (1803 –1873)

" Good teachers are costly, but bad teachers cost more."

Bob Talbert (1936 – 1999)

30
Intuition

Probably the most important attribute you must guard while pursuing a career in the arts is your intuition. Throughout your career you will have many friends and many adversaries, all of whom will have an opinion about who and what you should be, and both friend and foe are unlikely to be reticent in sharing their evaluations of you, sometimes in the most brutal ways imaginable. It takes real courage, resilience and most importantly self-awareness to hold onto and trust those attributes that make you unique.

The Collins dictionary defines intuition as knowledge or belief obtained neither by reason nor by perception. That definition makes intuition sound so flimsy and superficial as if to imply that intuition is, by its very nature, nothing more than a lot of hot air. And yet every great artist knows that their real power, creativity and individuality comes directly from intuition.

Many actors are pleasers, and having the capacity to please directors or casting agents is no bad thing providing that it is never at the cost of losing contact with that inner core, that inner self. So often I've seen auditions where actors have been prodded, kneaded, cajoled, harassed and sometimes intimidated into performing a particular piece in a certain way. In an effort to please, actors will often jump through extraordinary hoops to try and manufacture something akin to what the director wants. But unless an artist's intuition is allowed to breathe alongside whatever direction they've been given, that artist will never produce anything that will feel remotely authentic. Bullying an actor into an interpretation or performance is futile for a director and sheer insanity for an actor to comply with, because whatever is produced can never possibly be right. And remember, when it all goes wrong, it's likely to be the actor who takes the rap and not the director: all the more reason to protect and preserve your instincts at all costs.

That's not to say that all directors are bullies. In fact, the good ones never are. Direction and intuition can quite happily live together and the best directors know how to make that marriage work. But be cautious and vigilant in protecting your instincts. If you feel you are being driven into some belief or interpretation that does not ring true for you, then respectfully seek further clarification, further work, further rehearsal, further understanding before trying again because more often then not, truth lies smack dab in the middle of direction and intuition.

"Your time is limited, so don't waste it living someone else's life. Don't be trapped by dogma —which is living with the results of other people's thinking. Don't let the noise of other's opinions drown out your own inner voice. And most important, have the courage to follow your heart and intuition. They somehow already know what you truly want to become. Everything else is secondary."

Steve Jobs (1955 –)

"The creative is the place where no one else has ever been. You have to leave the city of your comfort and go into the wilderness of your intuition. What you'll discover will be wonderful. What you'll discover will be yourself."

Alan Alda (1936 –)

"Intuition isn't the enemy, but the ally, of reason."

John Kord Lagemann

"The mind can assert anything and pretend it has proved it. My beliefs I test on my body, on my intuitional consciousness, and when I get a response there, then I accept."

D. H. Lawrence (1885 –1930)

31
Breathe Like a Baby

When my son Ciaran was a baby, I vividly remember a time when he was banging away on our biggest soup pot with a wooden spoon and one of his own backswings caught him in the eye. He proceeded to let out one of the most powerful sounds on the face of the earth, a baby's cry! This is not a snuffling, crocodile kind of cry, but an earth-shattering, ear-piercing scream of pain! We've all heard it at some stage but have you ever wondered how babies are actually capable of doing it? If only I could get half of the actors I work with to breathe as efficiently and effortlessly as a baby! It's all about breath and release.

When a baby breathes in, their lungs are completely and effortlessly filled. This is because their upper bodies are upright and totally relaxed, and their air passages are unrestricted and fully open, capable of taking in the maximum amount of air in the quickest amount of time. When a baby's lungs are full, they release the air within them immediately and with varying degrees of velocity, depending on how badly they've scraped their knee or banged their finger. The whole process is simple, efficient, highly effective and doesn't cause vocal nodes.

So, the next time a director asks you to project more or sing louder, take a minute to think carefully on how a baby breathes when crying. Really observe and recognize the source of how babies make that magnificent and terrifying noise if just for the briefest of moments before running to them and kissing their ouches better. There's a lot to be learned out of the mouths of babes…

"It was he who impressed, time and again, the necessity of singing as nature intended, and –I remember –he constantly warned, don't let the public know that you work. So I went slowly. I never forced the voice."

Enrico Caruso (1873 – 1921)

"Breathing control gives man strength, vitality, inspiration, and magic powers."

Chuang Tzu (370BC – 201BC)

"There is one way of breathing that is shameful and constricted. Then there's another way; a breath of love that takes you all the way to infinity."

Rumi (1207 – 1273)

"Breathe. Let go. And remind yourself that this very moment is the only one you know you have for sure."

Oprah Winfrey (1954 –), O Magazine, September 2002

"I was not born to be forced. I will breathe after my own fashion."

Henry David Thoreau (1817 –1862), "Resistance to Civil Government"

"Everything in the world has a spirit which is released by its sound."

Oscar Fischinger (1900 – 1967)

"I wish you music to help with the burdens of life, and to help you release your happiness to others."

Ludwig van Beethoven (1770 –1827)

32
The Power of Stillness

Every great performing artist knows and utilizes the power of stillness. Stillness enables the power of our emotions and thoughts to shine out of us like a brilliant white light. Stillness allows our core, our soul, to soar out through our eyes and move mountains. Stillness cuts through chaos and noise like a samurai's sword. There is probably no greater tool an artist can possess than the power of stillness.

Take a minute to think about all the great dramatic moments you've witnessed or experienced on stage or screen. Stillness will most certainly have played a large part in the profundity of those moments. Stillness harnesses and channels our most burning passions and our most acute thoughts in a way that no other kind of physicality could. The sound and fury of our physical lives truly signifies nothing in comparison to a still body resonating so much more exquisitely.

Think of a cat stalking its prey. Is there any more powerful sight than a cat crouched low to the ground, moments before pouncing on their quarry, with its every muscle perfectly still and the intensity of its primal urges beaming out of its eyes? The slightest movement in one of the cat's paws tells volumes about the level of their anticipation for the kill, but once they pounce, the kill suddenly becomes coarse and clumsy. We humans aren't that different, in the sense that the greatness of our power can be observed most clearly when we are still.

So, the next time you're tempted to wag your head about like a dog while holding a long note, don't. Instead, be still and feel something. Or the next time you're tempted to wave your arms about or stomp your foot to demonstrate you're hurt, you mustn't! Be still and let your words and eyes tell us your pain. The power of stillness is that it conveys the biggest emotions with the greatest clarity. Learn it and use it!

"In peace there's nothing so becomes a man as modest stillness and humility."
William Shakespeare (1564 –1616), "King Henry V" Act 3 scene 1

"You do not need to leave your room. Remain sitting at your table and listen. Do not even listen, simply wait, be quiet, still and solitary. The world will freely offer itself to you to be unmasked, it has no choice, it will roll in ecstasy at your feet."
Franz Kafka (1883 –1924)

"I have discovered that all human evil comes from this, man's inability to sit still in a room"
Blaise Pascal (1623 –1662)

"We must learn to be still in the midst of activity and to be vibrantly alive in repose."
Indira Gandhi (1917 –1984)

"Never mistake motion for action."
Ernest Hemingway (1899-1961)

"A thought which does not result in an action is nothing much, and an action which does not proceed from a thought is nothing at all."
Georges Bernanos (1888-1948)

"There is nothing so useless as doing efficiently that which should not be done at all."
Peter F. Drucker (1909-2005)

"The most pathetic person in the world is someone who has sight, but has no vision."
Helen Keller (1880-1968)

33
Listen and Hear

If the audition panel decides to ask you to do something again, KEEP YOUR MOUTH SHUT, YOUR EYES FOCUSED AND YOUR EARS OPEN! It would take years to count the number of times I've asked an auditionee to try something differently, and they proceed to do it exactly the same way as before as if my words have completely washed over them. Oi vay! Countless times I've seen artists so eagerly searching for a perfect sycophantic or witty response that they've entirely missed the point of the direction they've just been given. Sometimes I see actors so busy checking out who's on the panel that they haven't looked at the person who's actually speaking to them. Or perhaps even worse, an actor puts on their 'listening face' when it is clear to everyone on the panel that they haven't understood a single word that's been said.

Unless you shut up, focus on the speaker and listen to their words, you don't stand a chance. And the tough bit is that you have to do all three simultaneously. First and foremost, how can you possibly understand the direction you're given if you're too busy being clever yourself? Shut up! Secondly, focusing on the speaker is crucial because so much of our understanding relies not just on words, but body language as well. Besides, when someone is speaking to you, giving them your undivided attention is just good manners and common sense. Thirdly, you have to listen before you can possibly understand. I've had candidates quiet as mice stare me straight in the eyeballs, feign the greatest of interest in what I'm saying, nod their heads enthusiastically at the profundity of my insights and then launch back into their number in exactly the same way! Two out of three ain't bad but it still won't work unless you're all ears!

We all want to work with people who can really listen, whether it's on the stage, in the rehearsal room or in an audition. Really listening and hearing direction requires calm and intense concentration, and your ability to comprehend and digest what is being said is fundamental to taking successful auditions. Don't allow your inner voices to annihilate the outer ones. Be still, focus, listen and HEAR!

"There are people who, instead of listening to what is being said to them, are already listening to what they are going to say themselves."

Albert Guinon (1863 – 1923)

"Really listening and suspending one's own judgment is necessary in order to understand other people on their own terms... This is a process that requires trust and builds trust."

Mary Field Belenky

"Listening to both sides of a story will convince you that there is more to a story than both sides."

Frank Tyger

"Opportunities are often missed because we are broadcasting when we should be listening."

Author Unknown

"So when you are listening to somebody, completely, attentively, then you are listening not only to the words, but also to the feeling of what is being conveyed, to the whole of it, not part of it."

Jiddu Krishnamurti (1895 – 1986)

34
Words, Words, Words!

Audition Panel:	Nice to meet you. What song have you prepared for us today?
Auditionee:	Mumble, Mumble, Mumble, Mumble
Audition Panel:	I'm sorry, did you say, 'I Dreamed a Dream?'
Auditionee:	Mumble, Mumble, Mumble, Mumble
Audition Panel:	OK, so could you please sing that for us now?
Auditionee:	blah blaaaah, blah blaah blah blaah, blah laaaaaaah…
Audition Panel:	Excuse me. We're really struggling to understand words. Could you try it again and really focus on your diction and the energy you're putting into the text?
Auditionee:	blah blah, blah Dream in time blah blaaaaaaaaah. When hope, blah blaaaah, blah life worth blah blaaaaah…

And so the sorry story of mumbling goes on and on and on…

In auditions as on stage, diction, the pronunciation of words, elocution, annunciation and projection are vital, and do not deserve to be pigeonholed as the domain of pedantic directors. Diction illuminates the underlying emotion of each word. Elocution gives significance, weight, and intelligence to each phrase. Annunciation inspires an appreciation for the beauty and rhythm of language. Projection ensures that every member of the audience feels what you feel.

I'd be a rich man if I had a dollar for every unintelligible lyric I've had to endure over the years. Unfortunately, most actors consistently underestimate the commitment they must make in theatre to the articulation of language. Many artists today make the very wrong assumption that because of modern technology and the widespread acceptance and usage of radio microphones, projecting diction is merely a practical issue that is solved though amplification. But words are the manifestations of our deepest thoughts, feelings, passions and inspiration. If we want what's inside our hearts and minds to be understood by an audience, then we must take the greatest of care with the shape, form and energy of each vowel and consonant. The sound and flavour of every word must be tasted, savoured, and experienced. The more poetically you relish each word's rhythm and articulation, the more we'll hear and understand as an audience.

"For me, words are a form of action, capable of influencing change."
Ingrid Bengis (1944 –)

"Speak properly, and in as few words as you can, but always plainly; for the end of speech is not ostentation, but to be understood."
William Penn (1644 –1718)

"Words —so innocent and powerless as they are, as standing in a dictionary, how potent for good and evil they become in the hands of one who knows how to combine them."
Nathaniel Hawthorne (1804 –1864)

"A word is not a crystal, transparent and unchanging, it is the skin of a living thought and may vary greatly in colour and content according to the circumstances and time in which it is used."
Oliver Wendell Holmes Jr. (1841 – 1935)

35
Persistence Pays

Overnight successes rarely exist in life, and the part that persistence plays in achieving success is rarely given its due. In most instances, the artists labelled 'overnight successes' have knocked on doors for years until the right door has opened at the right time. When persistence is fuelled by ambition alone or the desire to become famous, any success achieved will usually be fleeting. However, when persistence is fuelled by a burning passion for your craft and a self-belief that you can achieve greater and greater heights as an artist through training and hard work, then your ability to persist will be unstoppable. Every 'No' will be viewed as a momentary obstacle. Every failure will be used as a valuable lesson or tool that moves you onwards and upwards.

If you carefully examine the lives of the people you admire most, you will find that their pasts are littered with every conceivable obstacle and a myriad of 'No's!' After failing as a business man on two separate occasions, Abraham Lincoln unsuccessfully ran for public office seven times before finally being elected president of the United States. Thomas Edison had over 1000 failures before successfully patenting the electric light bulb. Walt Disney was on the verge of bankruptcy when he opened Disneyland. It's almost as if the size of their achievements is in relative proportion to the adversities they faced and the number of doors that were slammed in their faces.

Sometimes the difference between success and failure is simply your ability to persist and one of the most impressive things you can do as an artist is to keep coming back stronger each time, to keep knocking at those doors and taking those auditions, each time better than the last. The progress you make with each successive try will accumulate and snowball until it is eventually undeniable. Persist in all things and remember that nothing worth earning is ever easy.

"Let me tell you the secret that has led me to my goal. My strength lies solely in my tenacity."

Louis Pasteur (1822 – 1895)

"Nothing in the world can take the place of Persistence. Talent will not; nothing is more common than unsuccessful men with talent. Genius will not; unrewarded genius is almost a proverb. Education will not; the world is full of educated derelicts. Persistence and determination alone are omnipotent. The slogan 'Press On' has solved and always will solve the problems of the human race."

Calvin Coolidge (1872 – 1933)

"Never let your persistence and passion turn into stubbornness and ignorance."

Anthony J. D'Angelo (1972 –), The College Blue Book, 1995

"If I had to select one quality, one personal characteristic that I regard as being most highly correlated with success, whatever the field, I would pick the trait of persistence. Determination. The will to endure to the end, to get knocked down seventy times and get up off the floor saying, "Here comes number seventy-one!"

Richard M. DeVos (1955 –)

"The heights by great men reached and kept / Were not attained by sudden flight, / But they, while their companions slept, / Were toiling upward in the night."

Henry Wadsworth Longfellow (1807 – 1882)

"Aerodynamically the bumblebee shouldn't be able to fly, but the bumblebee doesn't know that so it goes on flying anyway."

Mary Kay Ash (1918 – 2001)

36
Live Long and Prosper

What is experience? One view is that it is simply the sum total of all the hard knocks and bumps that life spits out at us day in and day out. What doesn't kill you will make you stronger, right? But is that really true? Is it really fair to say that the crueller our life experiences are, the stronger and more resilient we become? I believe that most of what doesn't kill us actually wounds us deeply. It scars us and chips away at our self-esteem and confidence unless we have solid strategies in place so that the hard knocks of life don't leave us hardened to life. Walking out of an audition feeling ashamed, angry or humiliated because you have not hit that last note will have a huge knock on effect the next time you audition, unless you find ways of exchanging those negative emotions for ones that are ruled by logic and a sense of perspective.

Let me give you an example. Let's say that in your audition you missed that last high C but managed to get through the remainder of the song with no other problems. Many actors I know would leave that audition feeling embarrassed and angry with themselves because they couldn't reproduce in the audition what they achieved in the practice room. They missed the singular 'money note.' Tell me what industries you know of that consider a 99% success rate to be a failure. One note was problematic. Even if you proportion more significance to that one note compared to all the others, logic should tell you that you're still doing pretty damn well.

The same logic applies to the actual significance of that one particular audition. If you are taking the number of auditions you should be as a serious actor, you will have hundreds of auditions in you career. Why should one audition out of hundreds determine the outcome of all the others? It doesn't have to if you think about it rationally and logically. One audition where you don't hit the 'money note' is insignificant in the grand scheme of things. It doesn't matter in any way except as an opportunity to examine the experience and find ways to improve.

Artists are notorious for reacting illogically to facts. But if you place any importance on maintaining or indeed building your self esteem and confidence, think long and hard about employing a more objective and rational approach to evaluating your own performance. Logic is everything when it comes to self-appraisal. When reflecting on the success or failure of your performance in your next audition, make it your goal to think a bit more like Mr. Spock and bit less like Dr. McCoy.

"Only exceptionally rational men can afford to be absurd."
Allan Goldfein

"Learn the art of patience. Apply discipline to your thoughts when they become anxious over the outcome of a goal. Impatience breeds anxiety, fear, discouragement and failure. Patience creates confidence, decisiveness, and a rational outlook, which eventually leads to success."
Brian Adams

"People and things do not upset us, rather we upset ourselves by believing that they can upset us."
Albert Ellis (1913 – 2007) founder of Rational Emotive Therapy

"How hard it is, sometimes, to trust the evidence of one's senses! How reluctantly the mind consents to reality."
Norman Douglas (1868 – 1952)

"The words 'I am...' are potent words; be careful what you hitch them to. The thing you're claiming has a way of reaching back and claiming you."
A. L. Kitselma

37
Write It Down!

"I've got to rehearse my monologue, can you please shut up so I can concentrate?" you yell to your partner before leaving for your audition. On your tube journey into town the coughs and sneezes of a hundred infirm commuters seem to waft directly toward your vocal chords. In the waiting area of the audition, you have to stomach the incessant babblings and boastings of your colleagues whilst frantically trying to review your song lyrics in your head. In the audition itself, your inner voices won't shut up whilst the casting director's mobile phone continually buzzes on and off, on and off...... Distractions, distractions! They're everywhere and you must make them your sworn enemy. You must fight distractions at every juncture and hold onto your focus for dear life.

Easier said than done, right? What if I told you I know of one simple technique that is used by some of the most successful people on the planet to fight off every imaginable distraction and stay on track? Here it is. Decide on what your targets and goals are for each day and WRITE THEM ALL DOWN! There, I've said it. Decide on what your targets and goals are for each day and WRITE THEM ALL DOWN! I've said it again.

On the day of your audition I want you to meticulously write down every aspect of how you want the day to unfold. Here's a condensed version of one possible audition day diary; you'll get the idea.

- 8:00 –wake up –exercise –stretch –shower
- 9:00 –look up exact location of audition on map –organize, review and place in briefcase all audition material to be used (don't forget map, iPod, and spare CV) –choose and prepare all clothes for the day –pack scarf, hat, and umbrella just in case –prepare hot water, lemon and honey in flask and have ready by 11:00
- 11:00 –5 minute walk to train –listen to Bach on iPod for 11:18

train

- 12:00 —arrive at audition address —ten minutes meditation and stretch before going into building —eat snack —check in and find toilet —find private space for breathing exercises —stay loose —more breathing
- 1:00 —Audition – music, water, CV – stand tall, focus, listen, carpe diem!!!
- 1:15 —Exhale over a cappuccino

The simple but powerful act of writing down every task or goal you want to accomplish will enable you to stay focused and on track effortlessly, whether it's for an audition or an entire lifetime. Buy a notepad you can easily slip into your pocket or purse, WRITE EVERYTHING DOWN and replace it as soon as it's full. Consistently practice this one elementary exercise and it may prove to be the most important thing you ever learn.

Focus 90% of your time on solutions and only 10% of your time on problems."
Anthony J. D'Angelo (1972 –), The College Blue Book, 1995

"Science is organized knowledge. Wisdom is organized life."
Immanuel Kant (1724 – 1804)

"Don't agonize. Organize."
Florynce Kennedy (1916 – 2000)

"The overman...Who has organized the chaos of his passions, given style to his character, and become creative. Aware of life's terrors, he affirms life without resentment."
Friedrich Nietzsche (1844 – 1900)

38
I, Don Coyote

Knowing the style and story of the show you're auditioning for is fundamental to choosing the right audition material. How could you possibly choose the right material if you don't know what you're auditioning for? **Research!** Understanding the dramatic ebb and flow of your song as well as its context within the larger whole is key to delivering an intelligent and truthful audition. **Research!** Remember, it's entirely possible that someone on that audition panel will know whatever material you've chosen better than you. **Research!**

Intelligence can be a very useful thing. In this instance, I'm talking not about the 'smarts' kind, but the '007' kind. Discreetly use your own network to find out whatever you can about the forthcoming audition. Squeeze every morsel of information that you can from your agent about the audition – make them earn at least a little bit of their commission – for example who's on the panel, what each of them do, what you are being seen for, what age they are looking for, have they requested specific material? Ask, ask, ask and always independently check, in any way you can, that the information your agent has provided is correct – some agents are notorious for getting it wrong! What you find out may determine your ultimate fate. **Research!**

There is one audition I like to remember which illustrates the desperate lack of research some prospective candidates demonstrate and the catastrophic effect it can have on your subsequent career. It is the story of someone I'll call Joe. Joe came in to audition for Les Miserables, London with the song 'I, Don Quixote' from Man of La Mancha written by Joe Darion and Mitch Leigh.

Obviously a mate had suggested the song to poor Joe a little late in the day and I always envisaged him desperately listening to it on his ancient cassette player on his way in to the audition on the tube. When he walked out on stage, his first big mistake was to say he had lost his music on the tube and asked if he could sing it a cappella. Sadly for Joe, our pianist knew it and launched into its romping accompaniment which always reminds me of something you might hear out of a spaghetti western. Joe thought so too and heard the lyric title of 'I, Don Quixote' as 'I, Don Coyote!' To cut a long story short, when I run into colleagues on the street that were on Joe's panel that day, we can't help but immediately greet one another with the salutation of 'I, Don Coyote!'

Oh, by the way, although I still see Joe from time to time, he doesn't work much.

"Research is formalized curiosity. It is poking and prying with a purpose."
Zora Neale Hurston (1891 – 1960)

"What is research but a blind date with knowledge?"
Will Harvey (1967 –)

"The way to do research is to attack the facts at the point of greatest astonishment."
Celia Green (1935 –)

"Research is what I'm doing when I don't know what I'm doing."
Werner von Braun (1912 – 1977)

"The first step towards knowledge is to know that we are ignorant."
Richard Cecil (1748-1810)

"Some people will never learn anything, for this reason, because they understand everything too soon."
Alexander Pope (1688-1744)

39
Image Is King

There is absolutely no point in bitching and moaning about it: image is king! If you want to be in the entertainment industry you have to accept on some level that image is all-important. I've seen the most profoundly intelligent directors make the most acutely stupid casting decisions simply because an actor's muscles or curves were in all the right places. And then to my even further chagrin, seen those same 'mistakes' go out on stage and be extremely successful with audiences for the same reasons the director cast them in the first place – image, beauty, allure and glamour! Would a less beautiful but more intelligent performance have worked better? Very possibly not. Audiences will very often choose sex over substance and it's ultimately an extremely hard call for any audition panel to make when casting a production.

Personally, I have always found talent to be the most alluring quality an actor can possess, but every statistic under the sun bears out the fact that beauty wins over talent hands down. Statistically, beautiful children receive more love at home, beautiful students do better at school and beautiful adults win the best jobs and partners. Disgusting, isn't it? But important to know, particularly if you want to be a player in the entertainment game.

So, what's the answer? Become best mates with a plastic surgeon? Spend your last dime getting your nose fixed, teeth whitened, and fat liposuctioned? Well, I've got a simpler and far cheaper solution. I know it sounds obvious and takes discipline and hard work, but quite simply, exercise and diet improve everything to do with beauty: skin, weight, muscle tone, vitality, confidence and even glamour. Health is the core to beauty and allure.

Perhaps the day will come when you'll want to get those teeth whitened or the bump on your nose fixed. However, if you are physically in top form, whatever minor physical imperfections you possess will feel so much less significant to you and subsequently to everyone else.

So before you bemoan the injustice of the fact that 'Image is King,' make 'Health is King' your motto. Do everything in your power to be fighting fit to knock out all the bastards out there that cast with their glands rather than their brains.

"What the public wants is the image of passion, not passion itself."
Roland Barthes (1915 – 1980)

"The orgasm has replaced the Cross as the focus of longing and the image of fulfillment."
Malcolm Muggeridge (1903 – 1990)

"There is no excellent beauty that hath not some strangeness in the proportion."
Sir Francis Bacon (1561 – 1626), "Of Beauty"

"I'm tired of all this nonsense about beauty being only skin-deep. That's deep enough. What do you want, an adorable pancreas?"
Jean Kerr (1922 – 2003)

"Just because you are blind, and unable to see my beauty doesn't mean it does not exist."
Margaret Cho's weblog, 03-23-06

"Beauty isn't something on the outside. It's your insides that count! You gotta eat green stuff to make sure you're pretty on the inside."
Takayuki Ikkaku, Arisa Hosaka and Toshihiro Kawabata, Animal Crossing: Wild World, 2005

40
We'll Listen More If You Shout at Us Less

There's a famous story about Leonard Bernstein rehearsing with the New York Philharmonic when he was a young man. He stopped to speak to the principal clarinet player about a specific passage and waxed lyrical about what he felt the passage meant and what the composer had intended when he wrote it, hoping to inspire this musician to play the phrase better. Upon Bernstein finishing what had clearly been a rather moving and insightful observation, the cynical player replied to Bernstein in the hardest of Brooklyn accents: "So do you want it louder or softer?" Bernstein took in a deep breath and looked penetratingly into the eyes of this hardened musician's soul and simply said, "I want it louder and softer and everything in between!"

Artistry consists of a million different nuances, a million different colours whose sum total delivers an emotional charge, inspires our imaginations, or links us with the divine. How could you possibly think that coming into your audition and SHOUTING at us for 10 minutes would work?

The Irish say they can see 40 different shades of green in their stunning countryside. Can you imagine if there was only one shade of green, or one red, or one blue? How monotonous and dull would that make our world? Can you imagine if in your audition you expressed only one dynamic, one kind of inflection or one emotion?

So often I hear auditions where the candidate endeavors to wake us up and make us pay attention by delivering what I call a 'kamikaze audition.' This kind of audition can only have one kind of outcome and I suspect you know what it is. Strive for beauty of tone, clarity of words, and sincerity of emotion by using the most diverse and imaginative palette of colours and nuances. Give your thoughts and feelings artistic integrity and magic. Bottom line –**we'll listen more if you shout at us less!**

"A word is not a crystal, transparent and unchanging, it is the skin of a living thought and may vary greatly in colour and content according to the circumstances and time in which it is used."

Oliver Wendell Holmes Jr. (1841–1935)

"I cannot pretend to feel impartial about colours. I rejoice with the brilliant ones and am genuinely sorry for the poor browns."

Sir Winston Churchill (1874–1965)

"One should absorb the colour of life, but one should never remember its details. Details are always vulgar."

Oscar Wilde (1854 – 1900), The Picture of Dorian Gray, 1890

"If you're trying to take a roomful of people by surprise, it's a lot easier to hit your targets if you don't yell going through the door."

Lois McMaster Bujold (1949 –), The Warrior's Apprentice, 1991

41
Get a Sense of Humour

Find a song or monologue that makes you laugh, learn it and use it at your next audition. The vast majority of what we hear day in day out is full of pathos and pain. I can't tell you the sheer sense of relief when an auditionee comes in and delivers something that genuinely makes us laugh. Obviously, if you're auditioning for Hamlet, choosing a humorous monologue might not be the best first choice, but humour does tell us a lot about your sense of timing and your intelligence as an actor and can often be an effective weapon to perk up the eyes and ears of the audition panel and get you past that first round.

Develop your interest in observing the minute details or foibles of human behaviour that you might normally deem unimportant. There's probably no greater way of developing your comic observations than picking up and mimicking the little nervous ticks, the unconscious snorts or chortles, the pompous gestures, the annoying habits, the unique nuances of speech, dialect or accent that we all have as individuals. Often we can discover more about character by observing the periphery of human behaviour than anything else. The debris of human behaviour, the bits we know are there but we never really consciously noticed before are often the gems that help define character and make us howl with laughter. Knowing how to recognize and reveal the minutia of human foibles is a fun and effective tool to enhancing your range and effectiveness as an actor. Get a sense of humour!

"The most difficult character in comedy is that of a fool, and he must be no simpleton who plays the part."

Miguel de Cervantes (1547 –1616), Don Quixote, 1605

"Humour is the only test of gravity, and gravity of humour; for a subject which will not bear raillery is suspicious, and a jest which will not bear serious examination is false wit."

Aristotle (384 BC –322 BC)

"A sense of humour is part of the art of leadership, of getting along with people, of getting things done."

Dwight D. Eisenhower (1890 – 1969)

"Humour is everywhere, in that there's irony in just about anything a human does."

Bill Nye, Interview with Wired.com, April 2005

"Anyone without a sense of humour is at the mercy of everyone else."

William Rotsler (1926 – 1997)

"Laughter is the closest distance between two people."

Victor Borge (1909 –2000)

"Humour is an affirmation of dignity, a declaration of man's superiority to all that befalls him."

Roman Gary

"Humour is the great thing, the saving thing. The minute it crops up, all our irritation and resentments slip away, and a sunny spirit takes their place."

Mark Twain (1835-1910)

42
Don't Start Crying

Although I wouldn't say that auditionees crying before, during or after auditions is a common occurrence, it happens often enough in both sexes to warrant a mention because it is the cause of the tears that worry me. The stresses of taking an audition can magnify and intensify emotions or insecurities that might be lurking just under the surface. Once those inner demons start their negative chatter, it is often difficult to get them to stop unless we have specific strategies to silence them. Preparation, breath, tranquillity, diet, inner self esteem, physical health, baseline financial security and mental resilience are all key factors in making each subsequent audition you take more and more positive, regardless of the outcome.

How can any audition have a positive outcome if next month's rent depends on you getting the job? How can any actor view an audition positively if they have ripped their self-esteem to shreds before they even face the audition panel? How can any actor take an audition on four hours sleep after a hard night's partying? Time and time again I see actors putting themselves through what is, in itself, a challenging and very exposing process without having taken care of themselves, as human beings, first. And that's when the tears begin to flow...

I'd like to think that my colleagues and I take a more compassionate view towards someone breaking down in tears during an audition than, for example, the corporate world, but sadly the outcome will be the same in both situations. Ultimately, crying when you are seeking employment sends out all the wrong signals, and any empathy the audition panel shows on the day will be as human beings and not as employers.

For those of you who may contemplate using tears to solicit further attention or interest from the audition panel if things haven't gone to plan, I beg you to reconsider. This kind of drama is instantly transparent and the consequences down the line may be greater than you think. And for those of you that have allowed the stresses and strains of an audition to crack your shell and the tears have flowed, remember that the solution to this lies within you. Take action to take care of yourself and you'll find that the all the tears will dry up!

"Ready tears are a sign of treachery, not of grief."
Publilius Syrus (-100 BC)

"After twelve years of therapy my psychiatrist said something that brought tears to my eyes. He said, 'No hablo ingles.'"
Ronnie Shakes

"Laughter and tears are both responses to frustration and exhaustion. I myself prefer to laugh, since there is less cleaning up to do afterward."
Kurt Vonnegut (1922 –)

"Waste not fresh tears over old griefs."
Euripides (484 BC –406 BC), Alexander

"A woman wears her tears like jewelry."
Author Unknown

"To weep is to make less the depth of grief."
William Shakespeare (1564 – 1616), King Henry VI, 1589

"More grievous than tears is the sight of them."
Antonio Porchia, (1885-1968) Voces, 1943, translated from Spanish by W.S. Merwin

43
Offer Only What You Can Deliver

It is true that within each of us, there lies untapped potential which can blossom and flourish given the right inspiration, impetus and training. But in an audition, it is important that you and your CV accurately reflect what you can do on the day, and not what you hope to be able to achieve in a year's time. On the day of your audition, the panel might not have the time to fully explore things like total vocal range, dance proficiency, gymnastic ability, dialects, stage combat or other specialised skills. If they ask you if you can back-flip, don't say yes if you can't. Even if lying does secure you a recall, then what? You'll master a back flip within the next week? You'll probably just end up in hospital. 'Strong dancer' means something very different to 'strong mover,' and if you are a 'strong dancer' you should specify what your training consists of and what styles of dance are actually within your ability.

Do you really know what your vocal range is? When you say you can sing a high C, is that only whilst dancing on the table of your local watering hole after seven shots of vodka, or can you do it now in the audition? Conversely, if singing a high C is now a doddle for you and an E is securely in place, why doesn't your CV say so? If your belt only goes to a B natural, tell us! If you don't sing in your head voice, why do you call yourself a mezzo-soprano?

Does your photo accurately reflect you as you are today? If you are a 40 year old, 150-pound woman and the audition panel is looking at the photo of a 20 year old, 110-pound girl, why would you want to misrepresent yourself and waste your time and ours?

The reason this is so important is simply because time is precious to us all. Honesty and accuracy are important in any profession and in this day of digital technology, there are no excuses for you and your agent not to have a continually updated CV and photo. Equally, saying you can do something that you can't will simply make the panel feel their time is being taken for granted. Be proud of who and what you are today, make it your business to recognise your strengths and weaknesses objectively and offer only what you can deliver.

"There are people who exaggerate so much that they can't tell the truth without lying."
Mark Twain (1835 – 1910)

"We always weaken everything we exaggerate."
Jean Francois de la Harpe (1739 – 1803)

"Admit your errors before someone else exaggerates them."
Andrew V. Mason

"The game of life is the game of boomerangs. Our thoughts, deeds and words return to us sooner or later, with astounding accuracy."
Florence Shinn (1871 – 1940)

"If you tell the truth you don't have to remember anything."
Mark Twain (1835 – 1910)

44
Cynicism Kills

Unless you really make a determined effort to think rationally and logically about the imperfect world of auditions, it is so easy to allow one rejection after another to infect the enthusiasm and optimism you have for your chosen profession. So often, an audition is followed by an interminable silence where there appears to be no decision whatsoever. 'What's the matter with them? Can't they make up their minds?' Then when the call from your agent does finally come through, they say something vague like, 'Um, they didn't really feel you were right for the role.' What on earth is that supposed to mean?

The truth of the matter is that by the end of any audition process we will have seen a legion of wonderful artists, many of whom will sadly never receive any positive feedback and never fully understand how any multitude of reasons could have contributed to them not being recalled on this occasion. Sometimes the call back doesn't come for the simple reason that the jigsaw puzzle of casting changed (probably due to ongoing negotiations with an existing cast member) and the role they were just auditioning for is no longer available. It's equally true to say that often times we may love a particular actor and their work, but simply don't have anything available for them at the moment or perhaps our particular production doesn't quite match up with their individual talents. Will you ever really know accurately why you haven't been recalled? Probably not.

It is so important to always remember that the decisions any audition panel take are ultimately subjective, and that trying to hypothesize why you haven't received a call back is nothing short of pointless. Rationally know and accept that most of the feedback you'll receive will be vague and unusable and that the rejections you'll inevitably suffer may have little or nothing to do with your ability as an artist. But use this inescapable fact to your advantage. Logically make the decision to remain focused and optimistic about your next audition and always remember to let go of the past. Bitterness, cynicism, and jealousy are notorious bedfellows in our profession. They are totally counterproductive because once you allow this particular kind of ugliness into your consciousness, it will spread like a cancer through everything you do, no matter how hard you try to disguise it. Be watchful and protect your enthusiasm. Always work toward nourishing and replenishing the love you have for your craft.

"Cynicism is not realistic and tough. It's unrealistic and kind of cowardly because it means you don't have to try."

Peggy Noonan (1950 –)

"Success is the ability to go from one failure to another with no loss of enthusiasm."

Sir Winston Churchill (1874 – 1965)

"Think enthusiastically about everything; but especially about your job. If you do, you'll put a touch of glory in your life. If you love your job with enthusiasm, you'll shake it to pieces. You'll love it into greatness."

Norman Vincent Peale (1898 – 1993)

"Nothing great was ever achieved without enthusiasm."

Ralph Waldo Emerson (1803 – 1882)

45
Diversify

I can't say my heart bleeds when an actor tells me how terrified they become when asked to sing a song or learn a simple bit of choreography for an audition. They're terrified of course because outside of singing in the shower or dancing in a nightclub, they haven't got a clue! They simply haven't made the investment in time or money to prepare themselves for the absolute inevitability that at some stage of their auditioning career, a job will hang in the balance based on whether or not they can learn a dance routine competently or sing a song agreeably.

Actors that can't sing, dancers that can't act, singers that can't dance or any combination of the above are all equally exasperating, because unless you diversify as a theatre artist, you are seriously limiting your options for success. When I speak to the older generation of theatre performers out there, they constantly bemoan the fact that the young artists of today are often one trick ponies. In their day, unless you could deliver a joke, dance a number, sing a song and tell a good story you weren't considered a proper theatre artist. They simply can't understand the mindset of specialization when it comes to theatre.

The beauty of diversification in theatre is that each discipline nourishes and strengthens the other. When an actor learns how to sing well, they'll instinctively bring that newfound resonance into their speaking voice. When a dancer learns how to act skilfully, their ability to interpret and express choreography will be so much more potent. When a singer learns how to dance proficiently, their physical self-possession and poise will benefit to no end.

Of course no one can be best in all things, and your personal passions will inevitably lead you to focus on one discipline more than all the others. However, training and practice in all the diverse realms of theatre will ensure that you develop into a well-balanced and employable theatre artist. At the end of the day, diversification is just plain smart. If you want a long career in theatre, be an all rounder – you will never be out of work if you are a good dancer, solid actor and capable singer.

"Variety is the soul of pleasure."
Aphra Behn (1640 – 1689)

"I want all my senses engaged. Let me absorb the world's variety and uniqueness."
Maya Angelou (1928 –)

"Our minds are like our stomachs; they are whetted by the change of their food, and variety supplies both with fresh appetites."
Quintilian (35AD – 100AD)

"Hide not your talents, they for use were made. What's a sun-dial in the shade?"
Benjamin Franklin (1706 – 1790)

"Great talents are the most lovely and often the most dangerous fruits on the tree of humanity. They hang upon the most slender twigs that are easily snapped off."
Carl Jung (1875 –1961)

"We are all born with wonderful gifts. We use these gifts to express ourselves, to amuse, to strengthen, and to communicate. We begin as children to explore and develop our talents, often unaware that we are unique, that not everyone can do what we're doing!"
Lynn Johnston (1947 –), Lynn on Ideas

46
Make the Business Your Business

Staying current with your chosen profession ultimately has a lot to do with how you get through the door and how you manage to stay there. Make it your business to know what are the ground-breaking productions at the moment; who the most sought after directors are this year; what actors have been chosen for what awards; what long running productions are on the decline and what ones are being re-vamped; what shows are out on tour; which casting directors work for what companies; what agents have what clients; what new productions are about to be cast; what publications carry the best information on your industry; what websites give insider knowledge of what's currently happening in the business; what ticket agencies have the best deals on productions in your city...the list goes on and on and on.

Being informed is just plain smart. It shows your passion for your chosen career and your ambition for wanting to be a player within it. It means the next time a director chats with you, you'll have the knowledge to express your own observations and opinions about the current scene with confidence. See absolutely everything you can and push the boundaries of your current bubble of knowledge. If you love plays, go see the best new musicals. If you love musicals, go see the best new ballets. If you love rock music, go see a symphony. If you love opera, go to the best jazz club in town. Every experience will contain valuable lessons to be learned and new opportunities to be grasped. In London, most museums are free. Go to all of them! Discover how the visual arts have fed the dramatic and musical arts and vice versa over the entire course of history. By making the business your business, you'll be taking positive, practical steps toward claiming your right to be part of the profession you love.

"As a general rule the most successful man in life is the man who has the best information."

Benjamin Disraeli (1804 – 1881)

"I find that a great part of the information I have was acquired by looking up something and finding something else on the way."

Franklin P. Adams (1881 – 1960)

"Get the facts, or the facts will get you. And when you get them, get them right, or they will get you wrong."

Dr. Thomas Fuller (1654 – 1734), Gnomologia, 1732

"In your thirst for knowledge, be sure not to drown in all the information."

Anthony J. D'Angelo (1972 –), The College Blue Book, 1995

"The mind revels in conjecture. Where information is lacking, it will gladly fill in the gaps."

James Geary, The World in a Phrase: A Brief History of the Aphorism, 2005

"Where facts are few, experts are many."

Donald R. Gannon

47
Heroes

To appreciate and admire the abilities and accomplishments of another artist passionately is hugely important to your own development. Every time an artist miraculously reaches out and touches you profoundly, you'll find that a little bit of that magic stays inside of you. The more you seek out artists that have that power, the more you'll be able to recognize and understand how they make their magic and the more you'll want to possess that power yourself.

Heroes help us decide what qualities and personal characteristics we ourselves want to possess by venerating what is best in them. Heroes help us create and aspire to specific goals by marvelling at the height and scope of their accomplishments. Heroes give us vision and optimism for the future by admiring how they have overcome every imaginable obstacle. Some of you might need just one hero and some of you might need hundreds, but by celebrating your hero's achievements and personal virtues you help define a blueprint for developing your own character and talents.

When it comes to auditioning, choose audition heroes. Seek out examples of artists that actually enjoy the challenge of auditions. Try to model yourself after artists that fully accept and embrace the necessity of auditioning whilst ignoring the multitude of imperfections in the process. Copy the method and technique of actors that have a high success rate of call-backs. Once you've found these artists, make one or all of them your audition heroes. Success always leaves behind clues and by having audition heroes, you'll instinctively examine and decipher how they achieve their success. By admiring those who take auditions well, you will naturally identify and refine their techniques and adopt them for yourself.

But remember not to covet the trappings of your hero's success. Focus only on replicating their methods and the trappings will take care of themselves.

"How important it is for us to recognize and celebrate our heroes and she-roes!"

Maya Angelou (1928 –)

"A hero is no braver than an ordinary man, but he is braver five minutes longer."

Ralph Waldo Emerson (1803 –1882)

"We can't all be heroes because somebody has to sit on the curb and clap as they go by."

Will Rogers (1879 –1935)

"Nurture your mind with great thoughts; to believe in the heroic makes heroes."

Benjamin Disraeli (1804 –1881)

"Our heroes are people and people are flawed. Don't let that taint the thing you love."

Randy K. Milholland, Midnight Macabre, 09-27-07

"Old myths, old gods, old heroes have never died. They are only sleeping at the bottom of our mind, waiting for our call. We have need for them. They represent the wisdom of our race."

Stanley Kunitz (1905-2006)

"The legacy of heroes is the memory of a great name and the inheritance of a great example."

Benjamin Disraeli (1804-1881)

48
Work for Free

Whilst you're waiting to win that next crucial audition and become a star, why not do something that will inexorably propel you towards that goal: work for free!

"What! Work for free? You must be joking!" you say.

Come on now; don't tell me you're one of those silly people that knows the price of everything and the value of nothing. You just don't know all the benefits of working for free yet. Of course you can work for free! Don't be so jaded and faded! If you have enough money to survive and don't have a family to support, then get off your backside immediately and start working for free. The fee for your work may be nothing, but its worth is invaluable.

I can think of a thousand and one reasons why you should work within your industry for free, but I'll spell out just a few. First of all, the people who work for free in theatre are the passionate ones, the ambitious ones, the creative ones. This group contains the future directors, writers, choreographers, composers, filmmakers and stars of the industry. This group doesn't need payment in order to satisfy the fire in their eyes and the hunger in their belly. They live for the work and not the remuneration. Make this group your group. Secondly, what a fantastic opportunity to hone your craft, be courageous, try new ideas and make loads of mistakes without the pressure of a commercially-motivated producer on your back. Thirdly, new material is always work-shopped before being produced. The creative teams that put this material together are often the current movers and shakers in the industry. Participating in a workshop is the perfect chance to work with the best and brightest whilst making those crucial contacts which can open doors and create opportunities in ways you never imagined.

Sound pretty good so far? Are you convinced that working for free is a good idea yet? If not, then remember one absolute truth — if you don't use it, you'll lose it. Auditions are hard enough even when an actor is in top form. Working for free is the best way for a young actor to maintain and consistently improve their skills between auditions. Auditions are so much easier when they are in the context of ongoing work. Be active. Take part. Keep moving forwards. Work for free and auditions will start to feel like child's play, just as they should!

"My work is a game, a very serious game."
M. C. Escher (1898 –1972)

"The more I want to get something done, the less I call it work."
Richard Bach (1936 –)

"I'm a great believer in luck, and I find the harder I work the more I have of it."
Thomas Jefferson (1743 –1826)

"The reason why worry kills more people than work is that more people worry than work."
Robert Frost (1874 – 1963)

49
Relax

One might understandably think that the ability to relax should be something that is fundamentally simple to achieve. Take a hot bath. Have a cup of tea. Kick your feet up. Don't we all know how to switch off when we need to?

But the truth of the matter is that virtually every year we spend alive and kicking on this frenetic and chaotic planet of ours, our inability to relax multiplies exponentially unless we employ very specific techniques on a regular basis to combat the ever-increasing stresses and strains of modern day life. The profession of acting and the process of auditioning just happen to make finding those techniques to relax all the more imperative!

I think we all instinctively recognize how important relaxation is in the performance of any job, whether it's a television presenter, athlete, or actor. When relaxation is not at the core of a performance, a presenter's words sound stilted, an athlete's technique seems forced, and an actor's interpretation feels expressionless and empty. If our inability to relax is severe, then adrenalin can wreak havoc with our physiology to the point that it can completely destroy our ability to perform at all. So how can we simply switch relaxation on when endeavouring to perform in these extremely stressful situations?

I don't think the answer will come as a surprise, but its execution might prove more onerous than you had hoped. The answer, in a word, is practice. Practice meditation. Practice not taking drugs. Practice yoga. Practice not smoking. Practice regular exercise. Practice not drinking alcohol. Practice consciously slowing your heart rate down. Practice not drinking caffeine. Practice visualizing yourself remaining calm and relaxed in your auditions and performances. Practice healthy eating.

Practice BREATHING!!!

The more you practice relaxation techniques and the healthier your body becomes, the more you will be able to cope with the fright and flight responses that are triggered by the stresses of performance. How can you possibly hope to stay controlled in an audition if last night's bender is still lingering in your system? Your body is your instrument. Treat it like a Stradivarius and it will resonate and sing for you when and where you want it to.

"During [these] periods of relaxation after concentrated intellectual activity, the intuitive mind seems to take over and can produce the sudden clarifying insights which give so much joy and delight."

Fritjof Capra (1939 –) physicist

"This art of resting the mind and the power of dismissing from it all care and worry is probably one of the secrets of energy in our great men."

Captain J. A. Hadfield

"There is no need to go to India or anywhere else to find peace. You will find that deep place of silence right in your room, your garden or even your bathtub."

Elisabeth Kubler-Ross (1926 –2004)

"We spend most of our time and energy in a kind of horizontal thinking. We move along the surface of things…[but] there are times when we stop. We sit still. We lose ourselves in a pile of leaves or its memory. We listen and breezes from a whole other world begin to whisper."

James Carroll, O Magazine, October 2002

50
Get Cookin'!

One of the most frustrating things for any director to experience is after having given a direction, the actor replies, 'Well, so and so told me to do it this way and now you want something different?' Sacrilege! This is an outrageous response coming from the very person whose job it is to digest every seed of information they're given and to create a performance that is bigger and better than the sum of its parts.

Besides, it's entirely logical for actors to receive conflicting direction because every cause has an effect and every effect usually has a correction. Say, for example, the choreographer asks you to jump as high as you can on a particular cue. Then, when you do jump as high as you can, the director notices that you stand a good chance of being decapitated by a moving piece of scenery and asks you **not** to jump quite so high. Now as frustrating as this might feel at the time, is this really conflicting direction? At the end of the day, they've both asked you to jump in the same direction: up! You've responded to the first directive and jumped as high as you can, and there's been a subsequent correction from a different member of the team that has quite possibly saved your head. This cause, effect, correction continuum is rarely as simplistic as my analogy, but ultimately shares the same aim: to arrive at something that collectively works.

One of the most important abilities you can develop as an actor is to filter information. Like a human sieve, you must leave all the coarse material and opinion behind and create an end performance that contains the smoothest and most refined flavour of all the original ingredients within it. To do this successfully, it is vital to remember all the various stages of the filtering process so that each subsequent directive is treated according to its larger context. Just remember that whatever the hierarchy of the audition panel or creative team may be, each viewpoint will offer important vistas to admire and absorb. Like a good cook, use what you've got in the kitchen and get cookin'!

"You don't have to cook fancy or complicated masterpieces –just good food from fresh ingredients."

Julia Child (1912 –)

"Our days are a kaleidoscope. Every instant a change takes place in the contents. New harmonies, new contrasts, new combinations of every sort. Nothing ever happens twice alike. The most familiar people stand each moment in some new relation to each other, to their work, to surrounding objects. The most tranquil house, with the most serene inhabitants, living upon the utmost regularity of system, is yet exemplifying infinite diversities."

Henry Ward Beecher (1813 – 1887)

"There is only one way in which a person acquires a new idea; by combination or association of two or more ideas he already has into a new juxtaposition in such a manner as to discover a relationship among them of which he was not previously aware."

Francis A. Carter

"Life is a process of becoming, a combination of states we have to go through. Where people fail is that they wish to elect a state and remain in it. This is a kind of death."

Anais Nin (1903 – 1977), Winter of Artifice 1939

51
Space Invaders

Do you covet your personal space? Do you cringe when you're on a tube or bus and the bloke in the suit stands that little bit too close —so close in fact that you can smell his deodorant (or lack of it) and what he had for lunch? Sometimes even the ones we love are hard to face when sardined into an over crowded elevator. Personal space is something most of us cherish and when that line is crossed, communication and empathy on any level becomes strained.

Consider for a moment your next audition and what boundaries may exist in that environment. Consider the fact that on a long day, an audition panel may hear 12 auditions per hour for perhaps eight hours. Can you imagine why shaking the anxious, wet hands of 96 candidates each day whilst endeavouring to take accurate notes and deal with the administration of each audition might not be desirable for us? Even though most audition panels I've sat on would like to make you feel special — that all of the preparation, hard work, travel time and effort you've invested is hugely appreciated —it's quite simply a logistic impossibility for us to do that.

Now realise that when you come through that door, the audition panel will be sitting behind tables. On those tables lie stacks of CVs arranged into yes and no piles, as well as all our personal notes and comments with checks and crosses next to each name, marking each individual's fate on the day. If you come waltzing over to our table to shake each of our hands vigorously and greet us one by one, we would somehow need to protect the privacy of all the information that would be within your range of vision — an awkward moment for everyone.

Now let's imagine your audition has begun and you're standing two feet away from the front of our table. First and foremost, we need to see you, all of you, not just the spot on your nose. Secondly we may need to have a brief chat about you — that might prove awkward if you're within earshot. Standing so close to us that we can see your vocal chords vibrate won't allow us to determine if you can actually project your performance past the footlights. Give us some space so we can really look and listen objectively to your performance – it's in your best interest and ours to have a bit of professional distance and privacy. The second you walk through that door, find your space and claim it but be respectful of others – not a space invader!

"It is easy to be brave from a safe distance."
Aesop (620 BC – 560 BC)

"Keep five yards from a carriage, ten yards from a horse, and a hundred yards from an elephant; but the distance one should keep from a wicked man cannot be measured."
Indian Proverb

"Best wide-angle lens? Two steps backward. Look for the 'ah-ha'."
Ernst Haas, Comment in workshop, 1985

"You can learn as much –or more –from one glance at a private space as you can from hours of exposure to a public face."
Malcolm Gladwell (1963 –)
Blink: The Power of Thinking Without Thinking, 2005

"A penny will hide the biggest star in the Universe if you hold it close enough to your eye."
Samuel Grafton (1907 – 1997)

"There are two types of people--those who come into a room and say, 'Well, here I am!' and those who come in and say, 'Ah, there you are.' "
Frederick L Collins

52
Faith

You can research, you can practice, you can prepare, you can make ready, but sometimes the only antidote to fear is to simply have faith.

- Have faith that the worse case scenario is unlikely to unfold.

- Have faith that the audition panel desperately want you to do your best.

- Have faith that you've done everything in your power to prepare and it is now in the hands of the gods.

- Have faith that you'll breathe deeply and assuredly.

- Have faith your vocal chords will vibrate freely and irrefutably.

- Have faith the heel of your shoe won't break when you walk out on stage.

- Have faith your audition pianist will do his best to play your song beautifully.

- Have faith that you remember to take your music and bag with you after you finish your audition.

- Have faith that all the fabrications on your CV will go unnoticed or even better, unchallenged.

- Have faith that you look better than you feel.

- Have faith that you are one of a kind, worthy of respect, capable of greatness and likely to achieve it.

Aaaaaa....men!

"Faith is taking the first step, even when you don't see the whole staircase."

Martin Luther King (1929 – 1968)

"Where there is hatred, let me sow love. Where there is injury, pardon. Where there is doubt, faith."

Saint Francis of Assisi (1181 –1226)

"You must not lose faith in humanity. Humanity is an ocean; if a few drops of the ocean are dirty, the ocean does not become dirty."

Mahatma Gandhi (1869 –1948)

"Believe in yourself! Have faith in your abilities! Without a humble but reasonable confidence in your own powers you cannot be successful or happy."

Norman Vincent Peale (1898 –1993)

"If you think you can win, you can win. Faith is necessary to victory."

William Hazlitt (1778 – 1830)

"Getting ahead in a difficult profession requires avid faith in yourself. That is why some people with mediocre talent, but with great inner drive, go much further than people with vastly superior talent."

Sophia Loren (1934 –)

53
Networking

The single most difficult component of learning how to network is a psychological one. To make a conscious choice to move outside your comfort zone and seek out every opportunity to develop new contacts is a terribly difficult thing to do. It takes courage, effort and time to foster new personal and professional associations. Without a doubt, networking is one of the most underrated and underused skills an actor can cultivate toward expanding and promoting their careers.

The old adage of 'It's not what you know, but who you know' is founded on a substantial amount of truth. The business world has long recognized this and instead of being embarrassed by such aphorisms, they have openly embraced the idea that expanding your network of contacts is just plain good business. They have all sorts of organised networking events where entrepreneurs or business leaders come together with the express intention of working the room. They introduce themselves with their 'elevator pitch'- who they are and what they do in the time it takes to travel a few floors in an elevator –chat briefly, hand out their card and move on to the next person. It's all about selling the sizzle and not the steak.

Although far fewer organized events exist in the same way in our world, there are many lessons to be learned from the attitudes of the business community toward networking. If you take an active interest in our industry, you'll know when the right opportunities occur to meet new people in our profession. Many times these opportunities come in the form of opening night or industry parties and such events offer great possibilities to develop new contacts. Instead of drinking too much champagne, work the room; you'll ultimately have a much more interesting and productive evening. Find out who is likely to be at the party, do a bit of research so you have relevant things to say and develop your own version of an 'elevator pitch.' You could call it the 'look over your shoulder pitch' – the time it takes to say who you are and what you're doing before the luvvie you're speaking to looks over your shoulder to see who more important just walked into the room.

Being a good networker is about asking intelligent questions, being a good listener, responding passionately, offering something in return and not getting stuck. Move on and remember that although developing new relationships may or may not be beneficial in the short term, all it takes sometimes is that one encounter, that one meeting to open up doors you couldn't possibly have imagined. Happy networking!

"Contrary to general belief, I do not believe that friends are necessarily the people you like best, they are merely the people who got there first."

Peter Ustinov (1921 –2004), Dear Me (1977)

"If a man does not make new acquaintances as he advances through life, he will soon find himself alone. A man should keep his friendships in constant repair."

Samuel Johnson (1709 –1784)

"Never refuse any advance of friendship, for if nine out of ten bring you nothing, one alone may repay you."

Madame de Tencin (1682 – 1749)

"You can make more friends in two months by becoming interested in other people than you can in two years by trying to get other people interested in you."

Dale Carnegie (1888 – 1955)

"My mother used to say that there are no strangers, only friends you haven't met yet. She's now in a maximum security twilight home in Australia."

Dame Edna Everage (1934 –)

54
Individuality

When I hear an audition where the candidate's interpretation of a song is a virtual carbon copy of the Tony Award winning artist's performance on the original Broadway CD, I can't help but have an instant aversion to everything about them. I know I should try and lighten up and give them some sort of credit for at least taking the time to research what that artist's interpretation is, but to me that feels the same as congratulating an author for plagiarising someone else's work.

I can't help but think what a colossal waste of time it is for any artist to replicate a performance that firstly, is not your own and secondly, in some cases might be 25 years out of date. Doesn't it stand to reason that if that same Tony Award winning artist recorded that song today, 25 years later, they would have an entirely different interpretation of that song? Not only would they be 25 years wiser, but their dramatic and musical sensibilities would have inevitably evolved and changed. Why would anyone want to imitate and copy something that's already stylistically antiquated?

Perhaps even worse, what about auditionees that choose a song from an ongoing West End or Broadway production and then virtually duplicate the performance of the current artist singing that same song? How do you know the creative team for that particular production aren't counting the days until that artist leaves – perhaps that's why they're auditioning for the role in the first place!

Every possible argument should compel you to find your own voice, your own interpretation rooted in thorough research and emotional exploration. When you take the time to investigate the big picture, question everything that on first glance may seem self-evident and use your own experiences, intuition and intelligence to digest the text and interpret its significance on your own terms, then how can you fail to deliver something less than unique and individual? That's the audition we'll all be waiting to hear.

Imitation and replication are for amateurs. Individuality is how stars are born. Dig deep, listen intently to your inner self and discover your own path. Save listening to the CD until after you've won the job and finished the run!

"All Fords are exactly alike, but no two men are just alike. Every new life is a new thing under the sun; there has never been anything just like it before, never will be again. A young man ought to get that idea about himself; he should look for the single spark of individuality that makes him different from other folks, and develop that for all he is worth. Society and schools may try to iron it out of him; their tendency is to put it all in the same mold, but I say don't let that spark be lost; it is your only real claim to importance."

Henry Ford (1863 –1947)

"Always be a first-rate version of yourself, instead of a second-rate version of somebody else."

Judy Garland (1922-1969)

"How we remember, what we remember and why we remember form the most personal map of our individuality."

Christina Baldwin

"There is a vitality, a life force, an energy, a quickening, that is translated through you into action, and because there is only one of you in all time, this expression is unique. And if you block it, it will never exist through any other medium and will be lost."

Martha Graham (1894 –1991)

"Insist on yourself; never imitate... Every great man is unique."

Ralph Waldo Emerson (1803 –1882)

55
Enjoy

For every day you spend in this profession, you should take a moment to remind yourself how ridiculously lucky you are to call yourself a singer, dancer or actor. You don't have to work in a coal mine or on an assembly line, you consistently go against the flow of rush hour traffic and you earn a wage for being creative. Every day you'll learn new things, your colleagues will comprise of one of the most colourful collection of characters you'll ever find and you'll laugh a lot! Being an artist is a life long vocation instead of a part time career. Your life's work will give pleasure to other people like no other profession and at the end of the day, you're responsible only to yourself and your imagination. What an adventure!

However, although most people crave adventure, they don't cope with it very well when it's their only diet. Along with the highs that come with being an artist, the lows can be equally as extreme and here lies the danger. The stress and vulnerability of auditioning and performance cause many artists to experience depression and anxiety. Trying to stay optimistic and enthusiastic after a string of unsuccessful auditions, along with all the other associated problems, can be a real challenge.

If auditions begin to negatively influence your ability to stay positive and hopeful for the future then it's imperative you cast your mind back, and try to find that moment when you said to yourself, "This is what I want to do for the rest of my life! This is what I love most!" Every artist I know has had that same magical revelatory experience and equally, every artist I know will at some stage struggle to keep that memory alive. Take a moment to really remember and recommit yourself to that singular, uncompromising, passionate revelation, "This is what I **have** to do!" Write down in some creative way why you made the choice to dance, sing or act, and keep it somewhere close. Stay in touch with your greatest enthusiasms and you'll always be able to see the woods whilst enjoying noticing the trees!

"I finally figured out the only reason to be alive is to enjoy it."
Rita Mae Brown (1944 –)

"Enjoy your own life without comparing it with that of another."
Marquis de Condorcet (1743 –1794)

"Enjoy when you can, and endure when you must."
Johann Wolfgang von Goethe (1749 –1832)

"Never continue in a job you don't enjoy. If you're happy in what you're doing, you'll like yourself, you'll have inner peace. And if you have that, along with physical health, you will have had more success than you could possibly have imagined."
Johnny Carson (1925 –2005)

"I enjoy being a highly overpaid actor."
Roger Moore (1927 –)

"There is no cure for birth and death save to enjoy the interval."
George Santayana (1863 –1952), Soliloquies in England, 1922, "War Shrines"

"Roam abroad in the world, and take thy fill of its enjoyments before the day shall come when thou must quit it for good."
Saadi (1184 –1291)

"For believe me: the secret for harvesting from existence the greatest fruitfulness and greatest enjoyment is –to live dangerously."
Friedrich Nietzsche (1844 –1900), The Gay Science, section 28

56
Memory

Audition Panel:	What are you going to sing for us today?
Auditionee:	Um, well, aahh…(Runs over to the piano) let me just have a look at my folder…I seem to have drawn a blank…

The above scene plays out more frequently than you might think. Perhaps it's happened to you, where the second you walk through the audition room door you forget the title of the very song you've been frantically cramming into your brain in the corridor. Then the pianist plays the introduction and you forget the first page of lyrics.

If you're like most actors, if the embarrassment of drying doesn't completely destroy the rest of your audition, once you remember a few bits of text the remaining lyrics usually fall into place. One word or phrase connects to another and the story of the song suddenly clicks back into your memory banks. But very often, word associations and dramatic journeys are only formed haphazardly rather than being consciously organised – many artists just learn the song rather than consciously understanding what words take you where, when and how.

Sometimes just having an incredibly clear overview of the emotional journey of a song will be enough for lyric, melody and rhythm to be easily remembered. That's why it's incredibly important to make sure you understand all the facets and nuances of that journey before you begin to memorize. But if you find yourself still struggling, make further specific visualizations and associations.

What thought and series of words start the song? What's the last word of the 1st verse and how does it connect to the 1st word of the subsequent verse? Identify the structure of the song: how many verses does it have, where does the bridge fall, does it contain a chorus and how many times does it occur? Create a subtext for each phrase and memorize that sequence of ideas. Create a visualised physical journey that runs in parallel with your song lyrics and place one phrase in each location.

There are countless memory strategies and games out there to help you confidently remember and deliver those lyrics and tunes. Find out what they are and use them. Memory, like most things in life, can be improved and developed with practice. Developing a good memory should add another string to your bow in delivering self-assured and relaxed auditions.

"Study without desire spoils the memory, and it retains nothing that it takes in."
Leonardo da Vinci (1452 – 1519)

"Memory feeds imagination."
Amy Tan (1952 –)

"The secret of a good memory is attention, and attention to a subject depends upon our interest in it. We rarely forget that which has made a deep impression on our minds."
Tryon Edwards (1809 – 1894)

"Did you ever walk into a room and forget why you walked in? I think that's how dogs spend their lives."
Sue Murphy

57
Anything and Everything

Recently, I was sitting on a panel searching for possible Christine's for Andrew Lloyd Webber's Phantom of the Opera when a 40 year old, 200+ pound woman came into sing for us. In case you're one of the few humans on the planet who have not seen Phantom, the role of Christine is that of a young dancer who is plucked from the corps de ballet to star in the leading soprano role at the Paris Opera House, and not that of a middle-aged, pie eating alto who couldn't find a pair of point shoes large enough to fit over her swollen feet if she tried. Not that I have anything against 40 year old pie eating altos – I'm not far off that description myself, but I'm not auditioning for Christine for god's sake. The woman in question had a perfectly respectable voice but didn't seem to have any respect for herself or us. Did she honestly think that her talent was such that for the first time in 20 years of casting Christine's, we were going to go for an overweight middle-aged alto?

Presuming she was of a generally sound mind, perhaps she thought that even if she were not ideal for the role of Christine, by attending the audition she would automatically be considered for other roles or other productions? NO! We can only presume she has no understanding of the requirements of the role, no respect for our time and no, we will not be considering her for other roles because she is quite possibly insane. Her agent, who obviously hadn't met with their client for the last ten years and who is also quite possibly insane, received a nasty phone call from our casting director for having been sent a headshot and CV that resembled Michelle Pfeiffer more than the Mama Cass we had the pleasure of meeting.

Knowing your weaknesses is just as important as knowing your strengths. Do everything you can to support and promote your strengths, but for god's sake, know what you can't and shouldn't do and keep it to yourself. Know what you're auditioning for and don't compromise your own sense of self by mindlessly auditioning for anything and everything.

"Genius may have its limitations, but stupidity is not thus handicapped."
Elbert Hubbard (1856 – 1915)

"The only way most people recognize their limits is by trespassing on them."
Tom Morris (1960 –)

"Better a cruel truth than a comfortable delusion."
Edward Abbey (1927 – 1989)

"Givers have to set limits because takers rarely do."
Irma Kurtz (1936 –), Cosmo Magazine, September 2003

"When all else fails, there's always delusion."
Conan O'Brien (1963 –)

"The final delusion is the belief that one has lost all delusions."
Maurice Chapelain

58
Pianists

To use or not to use your own audition pianist; that is the question.

Each producer will have different resources and differing capabilities to provide audition pianists. The top producers usually have the best pool of audition pianists and will spend a significant portion of their audition budget making sure they have someone who knows the repertoire, sight reads extremely well and is a technically solid player for their auditions. This group of pianists are a rather elite bunch and the smaller or newer producers may find it extremely difficult to provide a top player for their auditions. Some may not even realize how important it is for the success of their own casting. For that reason alone, take the time to investigate the company you're auditioning for and assume the worse if it's a small or new producer.

The next question is of course; can you afford to use your own pianist? If the answer is yes, then by all means go ahead, especially if your material is outside the standard repertoire, technically difficult or contains many tempi changes. But here's the rub. Using your own pianist is potentially dangerous for the following reason: whom you use is ultimately a reflection on you. It shouldn't be, but it is.

If you walk in to your audition with a pianist that looks like Richard Claderman and plays like Liberace or vice versa, you'll likely end up being upstaged by your own accompanist. Also, if you do happen to audition on the day that the local boy genius is playing for auditions, and you bring in someone who plays with their knuckles by comparison, again the panel's attention will be diverted to your idea of Marvin Hamlisch instead of you.

If you think about the psychology of it, all day long for better or for worse there's a level playing field and then you, all of a sudden, introduce into that environment a new element. Regardless of your pianist's technical prowess, a certain degree of attention which should be focused on you will now inevitably be focused on someone else. That's why I usually recommend that unless your material is notoriously difficult to play or sight read, go it alone.

Ultimately before you decide, always run your music by a pianist that's in the business in order to get an idea whether your chosen number is off the Richter scale of difficulty. If you do decide to use your own pianist, make sure they're bloody good. Or even better, use someone who is already in that elite audition pianist pool and happens to be free on the day.

Oh, by the way, just one final bit of advice. If you do make the decision to go it alone and use the pianist provided for you, treat him or her like they are the brother or sister you always wished you had. They are absolutely the closest thing to a friend you have in that room.

"When she started to play, Steinway came down personally and rubbed his name off the piano."
Bob Hope (1903 –2003)

"The piano is a monster that screams when you touch its teeth."
Andre Segovia (1893 –1987)

"The piano has been drinking, not me."
Tom Waits (1949 –)

"There are more bad musicians than there is bad music."
Isaac Stern (1920 –2001)

59
G.I.G.O.

Garbage In –Garbage Out! If reading GQ or Cosmo is the apex of your intellectual stimulation, your ability to articulate your thoughts and ideas intelligently will be extremely limited. Whatever you body consumes will determine your general health and confidence levels. If alcohol and cigarettes are the staples of your diet, your ability to perform in stressful situations will be dramatically impaired. Whatever you feed your soul will ultimately determine what kind of artist you become. If you don't seek out performers and performances that inspire and touch your spirit, you will never be able to communicate profoundly with an audience. Garbage In – Garbage Out.

Let me tell you a tragic little story I see happen time and time again that relates to G.I.G.O. Talented boy graduates from drama school. Boy takes a few auditions and has a bit of success. Boy is offered two jobs: play the leading role in a budget regional tour, or take an ensemble role with covers with an experienced cast in a first class production in the West End. Boy decides to be a big fish in a little pond and takes money and the tour. Two years later, boy meets girl in London and decides he now wants to be a big fish in a big pond too. Problem is that boy has now had two years of G.I.G.O. and is a bit too fat and drowsy to compete with all the other big fish. Boy can't find work. Boy loses girl. Boy never works again. I told you it was a tragedy.

When you choose to surround yourself with mediocrity, some of it is bound to rub off. Surround yourself with the best in the industry and you'll become one of them. The day will inevitably come when your banker will decide that taking that lead role on the budget tour is in your and his best interests, but until such time, work toward establishing a resilient foundation of experience and skill from which you stand a fighting chance of surviving that inevitable onslaught of mediocrity.

"Because everything we say and do is the length and shadow of our own souls, our influence is determined by the quality of our being."

Dale E Turner (1917 – 2006)

"In the beginning you must subject yourself to the influence of nature. You must be able to walk firmly on the ground before you start walking of a tightrope."

Henri Matisse (1869 – 1954)

"Be around the people you want to be like, because you will be like the people you are around."

Sean Reichle

"With regard to excellence, it is not enough to know, but we must try to have and use it."

Aristotle (384 BC –322 BC), Nichomachean Ethics

"Be a yardstick of quality. Some people aren't used to an environment where excellence is expected."

Steve Jobs (1955 –)

"Excellence is an art won by training and habituation. We do not act rightly because we have virtue or excellence, but we rather have those because we have acted rightly. We are what we repeatedly do. Excellence, then, is not an act but a habit."

Aristotle (384 BC –322 BC)

60
Embrace Your Imperfections

Because most artists strive to create an experience that transcends the ordinary or banal, many of the most destructive characteristics of perfectionism often become part of the artist's psyche. The unrealistic and irrational refusal to accept anything less than perfection simply sets one up for a cycle of one failure after another because at the end of the day, we are all human beings – capable of greatness, but never perfection. Imagine the long term, self-inflicted psychological damage that comes from constantly measuring yourself against standards that are unattainable. Human beings are capable of achieving what is excellent, precise and sublime, but never perfect. Think about the actor who, after each audition or performance, reviews and relives every imperfection. This kind of negative visualised playback simply chips away at one's confidence and reinforces every flaw, until such time that fear of failure will paralyse them into non-participation.

It's important to realize that imperfection and success actually work hand in hand. It's only through being imperfect that we learn to work smarter and grow wiser. Every time human beings perform, some level of imperfection is not only inevitable, but an incredibly important part of achieving future success. Quite simply, without imperfection it is impossible for you to become the artist you want to be. By accepting and welcoming your humanity, you allow your body to work freely and intuitively. When you measure yourself by impossible standards, your body will work mechanically and artificially. By embracing your imperfections and accepting that it is only through your mistakes that your performances will grow and improve, you will find that you will sense the experience of performance as it unfolds, rather than observing and directing it from outside your body. Simply put, perfectionism makes us try too hard or 'choke.' Leave perfectionism to God and programme your mind to equate imperfection with success.

"Remember that fear always lurks behind perfectionism. Confronting your fears and allowing yourself the right to be human can, paradoxically, make you a far happier and more productive person."

Dr. David M. Burns

"Perfectionism is simply putting a limit on your future. When you have an idea of perfect in your mind, you open the door to constantly comparing what you have now with what you want. That type of self criticism is significantly deterring."

John Eliot, Ph.D. (1972 –) Reverse Psychology for Success

"Artists who seek perfection in everything are those who cannot attain it in anything."

Eugene Delacroix (1798 – 1863)

"I am careful not to confuse excellence with perfection. Excellence, I can reach for; perfection is God's business."

Michael J. Fox (1961 –), quoted by Lorne A. Adrain in 'The Most Important Thing I Know'

"I don't confuse greatness with perfection. To be great anyhow is…the higher achievement."

Lois McMaster Bujold (1949 –), Mirror Dance 1995

"The idea of perfect closes your mind to new standards.. When you drive hard toward one ideal, you miss opportunities and paths, not to mention hurting your confidence. Believe in your potential and then go out and explore it; don't limit it."

Dr John Eliot (1972 –), Reverse Psychology for Success 2009

DANIEL BOWLING

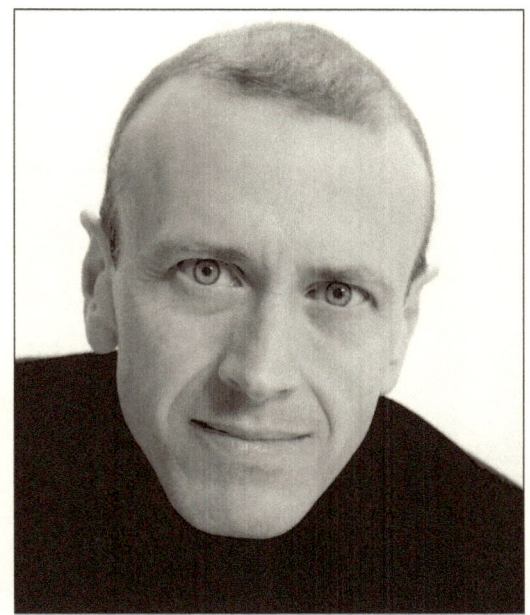

Photograph by John Paul Holton

Daniel Bowling has been a music supervisor and music director for Cameron Mackintosh Ltd for the last dozen years and during that time contributed to many of the CML stable of London and touring productions including The Phantom of the Opera, Les Miserables, Miss Saigon, Cats, Mary Poppins, and Avenue Q. He has had a long association with Cats worldwide and launched productions from Moscow to Madrid. He is currently music director for the hugely successful London production of Joseph following on from the BBC television series Any Dream Will Do.

Daniel graduated from The Curtis Institute of Music in Philadelphia and continued his studies at the Julliard School and St. Louis Conservatory of Music. His conducting teachers include Leonard Bernstein, Michael Tilson-Thomas, Sergio Celibidache, Charles Bruck and Max Rudolph.

www.ingramcontent.com/pod-product-compliance
Lightning Source LLC
Chambersburg PA
CBHW030812180526
45163CB00003B/1244